THE HOUSE OF NAHYAN

ALSO BY *James Edmonds*

FICTION
The Declining Day
Ozymandias
The Start of Something New
The Immolation
Dead Stars
Berenice

NONFICTION
American Master: A Portrait of Gore Vidal
King Faisal: A Life
The House of Nahyan
Boobocracy: Essays and Reflections
Cosmicommunist: Essays on Calvino

The House of Nahyan

The Story of an Arabian Dynasty

James Edmonds

Copyright © 2017, 2019 by James Edmonds
All rights reserved. No part of this book may be reproduced, scanned, or distributed in any printed or electronic form without permission.
First Edition
Printed in the United States of America
ISBN: 9781717803184

CONTENTS

The Sands
1

Gazelles
8

Daggers
16

Brothers
27

Horizons
46

Unities
62

Schisms
81

Vultures
103

Hawks
124

Whirlwinds
140

The House of Nahyan – Selected Family Tree
Bibliographical Note

THE SANDS

WILFRED THESIGER LIVED a life of his own choosing and one of those unorthodox choices brought Thesiger, one of the last "Victorian" explorers, to southeastern Arabia. The Oxford-educated adventurer and walking anachronism got a job in what later became the United Nation's Food and Agricultural Organization's anti-locust unit. Thesiger had no interest in locust movements or breeding grounds; rather "they provided me with the golden key to Arabia." Thesiger was very English – tweed-jacketed and campily clipped of vowel – but he was also the antithesis of the typical English gentleman. He possessed a deep, passionate attachment to other cultures and had no illusion that his society, his future, was best.

Between 1945 and 1949 Thesiger crossed and re-crossed the Empty Quarter, the 250,000 square miles of desert that stretch from southwest of Abu Dhabi into Saudi Arabia and Oman. The Bedu called it al Rimal, the Sands. Thesiger called it a "bitter, desiccated land that knows nothing of gentleness or ease." In the summer, temperatures soared to 150 degrees and easily exceeded 100 in winter. The region's harshness defies permanent human habitation. Bread was baked in the sand and so constantly covered in it. Water was rare and so brackish that camels would refuse it at times.

"The everyday hardships and danger, the ever-present hunger and thirst, the weariness of long marches: these provided the challenges of Bedu life against which I sought to match myself, and were the basics of the comradeship which united us." Thesiger dressed as they did and adapted his classical Arabic as best he could. The Englishman's guides, Salim bin Ghabaisha and Salim bin Kabina, two teens from the Rawashid tribe, accepted "the Christian" as one of their own, naming him Mubarak bin London – " the blessed one from London" – and taught him the ways of the desert and of the tribes.

He grew to love the "barbaric splendor" of the traditional way of life of the Bedu. He fell in love with the people – their nobility, hospitality, discipline, patience, loyalty, resourcefulness – and most of all the timelessness of their world. The Bedu accepted him because they believed he understood them, at least so far as possible for a European. Thesiger also fell in love with the beauty of the harsh wilderness. He recalled sitting atop a high dune and being overpowered by the scenery. "It was very still," he wrote, "with the silence which we have driven from our world." This he thought was far superior to the bustle of cities with their automobiles and easy luxury.

Thesiger was the third Englishman to cross the Empty Quarter but he was the first to make detailed maps, the first to visit the Liwa Oasis, the first to cross part of the Umm As-Sammim – "the mother of poisons" – an area of treacherous Omani quicksands where people, camels, and herds of animals disappeared.

On April 7, 1948, Thesiger, amidst his second crossing of the Sands, rode his camel into the settlement that is today called Al-Ain. His party approached the settlement from Abu Dhabi and traveled through the red sand dunes that still protect the town on that side.

"... We approached Muwaij'ei, one of the eight small villages in the Buraimi oasis. It was here that Zayed (sic) lived. As we came out of the red dunes on to a gravel plain I could see his fort, a large square enclosure, of which the mud walls were ten feet high. To the right of the fort, behind a crumbling wall half buried in drifts of sand, was a garden of dusty, ragged palm trees, and beyond the palms the isolated hog's back of Jebel Hafit (sic) about ten miles away and five thousand feet high. Faintly in the distance over the fort I could see the pale-blue outlines of the Oman mountains..."

Thesiger was eager to meet Zayed. He was no soft townsmen but a true Bedu at heart and one whose "great reputation" had spread among the tribes that roved the Sands all the way down to Arabia's southern coast. Thesiger asked a bystander to take him to the sheikh. The man pointed to a thorn tree, about thirty yards away, in front of the fort. A group of men sat beneath it, with Zayed at their center. He was "sitting" – holding a majlis where anyone could come and talk with him. Zayed received them with great hospitality, for life in the desert was lived in perpetual anticipation of guests.

I greeted them and exchanged the news with Zayed. He was a powerfully built man of about thirty with a brown beard. He had a strong, intelligent face, with steady, observant eyes, and his manner was quiet but masterful. He was dressed, very simply, in a beige-colored shirt of Omani cloth, and a waistcoat which he wore unbuttoned. He was distinguished from his companions by his black head-rope, and the way in which he wore his head-cloth, falling about his shoulders instead of twisted round his head in the local manner. He wore a dagger and a cartridge belt; his rifle lay on the sand beside him. I had been looking forward to meeting him, for he had a great reputation among the Bedu. They liked him for his easy informal ways and his friendliness, and they respected his force of character, his shrewdness, and his physical strength. They said admiringly, 'Zayed is a Bedu. He knows about camels, can ride like one of us, can shoot, and knows how to fight.'

Zayed bin Sultan Al-Nahyan ruled six of the villages in the Buraimi Oasis; the other two acknowledged the Sultan of Muscat as their lord. Zayed was the *wali*, or representative, of his brother Shakhbut, the ruler of Abu Dhabi. He worshiped Allah and loved the desert and within two decades would become one of the richest men in the world. One whose name would be remembered and worshipped.

Thesiger would stay with Zayed for a month. For a month, he "sat" with him, outside the fort, as Zayed heard complaints from tribesmen, be they Bani Yas, Manasir or Awamir. He watched him mediate disputes, mostly over camels, and offer judgment, for he had a reputation for justice. Usually a notorious outlaw, sometimes even sitting in the circle, had stolen some animals. Zayed preferred to have the outlaws at his fort rather than at a rivals' fort or roaming free.

The camel, of course, was a lifeline in the desert and the Bedu took more care of them than themselves. They could live from its milk for days when hard-pressed and the location of camel shit told them where the beast had last grazed and drank water. Some Bedu could tell the camel's tribe by reading its tracks.

Thesiger returned to Buraimi that winter in time for the hawking season. Over coffee one evening, Zayed insisted he accompany them on the hunt. Thesiger leapt at the chance and eagerly observed Zayed readying camels, ordering provisions, and feeding and branding new peregrine falcons with his mark. They would spend a month hunting together on Jebel Hafit and in the sands around the villages and formed a close, lasting friendship.

Every day in the middle of that vast nothingness, the Arab hunters searched for the houbara bustard, a bird that half flies and half runs from the winter wastes of Iran and Iraq to the warmer and more pleasant wastes of the Persian Gulf.

In 1929 HRP Dickson described the houbara's yearly arrival on the Arabian Peninsula as "a season for rejoicing." He wrote, "The rains are close at hand and...the houbara have arrived. They are verily, like the manna of old Allah's reward to those who have endured the summer heat."

The houbara had been a fascination to the great desert sheikhs for hundreds of years. Poems had been composed about it and old men of the desert sung of it. The houbara is a clever, wary bird and part of the allure was in finding it. One could spend half a day following its tracks. It was a contest of wits. Then there was the contest between the two birds. The sheikhs said that the houbara was the ultimate challenge for the falcon. Much of the fascination was in the flight, which could go on for miles. Hunter and prey are both fast. The houbara tries to stay on the ground, where it is difficult, sometimes impossible, for the falcon to strike. Meanwhile, the falcon tries to cajole or frighten it into the air. There the falcon reaches for the sun, then comes down on the houbara. Yet it must always stay above or else the houbara, seemingly as part of its defense apparatus, emits a dark green slime violently from its vent. The slime could temporarily blind the falcon or glue its wings together, rendering the hunter unable to fly. Once that happened many falcons would never hunt the bustard again.

Islam means submission to the will of God. In the desert, there is little else you can do but submit and pray for God's mercy. There on a dune in the middle of nowhere Zayed would bow his head to the ground. Submission makes everyone equal. A ruler like Zayed is no different from other men in the sight of God. He submits like them, and wherever he is he prays like them, and with them too. Five times a day, from dawn to dusk.

Thesiger arrived in Arabia "just in time." In his five years there, he traveled approximately ten thousand miles by camel. It turned out that he was a last witness to a world that has utterly disappeared. He knew what would happen.

With the oil prospectors roaming around, change was destined to come. It was only a few years before oil wells would become more common than oases and the Bedu would abandon their desert wandering for a comfortable, if humdrum, life in the towns. It would be only a few years before Thesiger's friend Zayed would be torn between two worlds; oil would allow him to erect a new nation on those sands. Islam and hospitality would remain constant but everything else would change. Zayed was born in an old Arabia but would die in a new one.

GAZELLES

THESIGER WAS ONE of a generation of sand-mad Brits who went native in the Arabian desert and around whom hovers a gust of fantasy, sexual perversion and nihilism. "I wanted color and savagery," Thesiger declares, "a cleanliness which was infinitely remote from the world of man...I craved for the past, resented the present, and dreaded the future." In Arabia, Thesiger and those who came after him would find all of those qualities in abundance.

Taking out an old map I plot a triangle – the same rough passage that Abu Dhabi's people used to follow from the coast to the mountains flanking Al-Ain and the southwestern deserts at the edge of the Empty Quarter, and the Liwa, a sprawl of oases that marks the start of the great ocean of dunes to the southwest. This is where the Bani Yas, the tribal confederation that founded Abu Dhabi, sprang from.

Pastoral people drifted back and forth across Arabia more than 9,000 years ago when the land was more fertile and the climate temperate. Even after the bountiful idle that ended in the third millennium BC and the temperature warmed to today's searing heat, many people continued to come. Migrating waves spread up from southern Arabia to settle the Buraimi Oasis – the site of modern Al-Ain in the fertile shadows of the Hajar Mountains – cultivating enough land to support a permanent community. Later herdsman of the Bani Yas inched down from the Najd, the large plateau at the center of modern Saudi Arabia, toward the Dhafrah area in the southwest of Abu Dhabi in search of grazing lands. They settled around the Liwa crescent of oases. It is from them that many of today's tribes are descended.

For the new settlers, the prospects were not auspicious. In a barren terrain, they were forced to eke out a living grazing livestock and breeding camels, bringing settled people what they did not have. Those who lived by the sea traded dried fish to the interior or became pearlers. In the hinterland people kept animals and grew dates, fruits, and grains, selling the dates and stacks of kindling wood to those on the coast, where vegetation was scarce. Some raided far off villages for livestock, camels and people, who could be traded as slaves to anyone who would buy them. The Bedu tribes provided their camels as beasts of burden to those coming to and from Buraimi and the Liwa and led caravans across the dunes with the turn of every season. Since goods required transporting across the terrain and families always traveled in groups, hoping their numbers would intimidate bandits, the camel trains became indispensable.

Over the generations, the settled and nomadic seemed to trade places as fortunes waxed and waned, and tribes learned to work for mutual benefit. Wandering was a necessity; even settled people moved with the seasons to accommodate the climate and the shifting opportunities for subsistence. They dispersed for winter and spring to the desert with their camels or down to the coast, fishing and preparing for the grueling pearling season.

They gathered for the summer in the Liwa or Buraimi Oases, where the water was fresh, and there was shade, dry air, dates and other crops to harvest. These people – around 70,000 of them – lived opportunistically, suspended in the present. Pearls were exchanged for cloth, tallow for candles, soap for foodstuffs, tools and, from the eighteenth century, antiquated firearms. Along with his camel, a rifle was a treasured possession for any tribesman.

At sea, they followed the stars and the sun. In the sands, they read the ground for signs of life. A carpet of brilliant flowers signified that the wadis on higher ground were flowing. The houbara flying south brought winter cool and the chance to use tamed falcons in the hunt. Superstition and desert folklore attributed aphrodisiac qualities to its meat, the taste of which vaguely resembled turkey. Men would hunt the houbara until the migration dwindled to almost nothing in the 1960s. On the ground some used Salukis for hunting hare and arrows or guns for the Arabian gazelle. Killing wild creatures was preferable to sacrificing valuable domestic livestock. Since no one could be sure there would be food and water the next day, the future was not worth speculating about. "A drop of dew is as paradise for a palm tree," or so the saying went.

In the crescent of oases around Liwa, stretching in an arc formation for about seventy miles west to east in the southernmost portion of modern-day Abu Dhabi, the forty or so allied tribes that came to form the Bani Yas expanded their *dar*, or territory, through strategic arrangements with independent houses such as the Manasir, Dhawahir, and Awamir to boost fighting numbers and keep a watchful eye over the land. They were not a hardened warrior people. In the tough terrain, the rooting out of enemies was only done through force of circumstance. War usually took the form of a *ghazzu*, or raid. Tribesmen would swoop down on an enemy village or encampment and seize camels, goats, and people before escaping back into the anonymity of the desert. Smaller clans were happy to enjoy the protection of belonging to a larger, more formidable group and over the generations they created a loose alliance to ward off opponents from hostile quarters such as Qatar and Muscat.

Diverse in spirit and skill, the many tribes supported each other to maintain supremacy, or at least independence, through the times of conflict and celebration. The Rumaithat settled on the coast, dedicating themselves to fishing and pearling; the Mazari were dedicated to the desert; the Qubaisat tribesmen had date gardens in Liwa before favoring maritime activities. Along with the Mazari and several others, the Al Bu Falah spent winters in the desert grazing their camels. Many of the Al Bu Falah also spent summers on the coast pearling. When the Dhawahir, veteran date cultivators from Buraimi, came under their control in the nineteenth century, a settled element was added to the tribal population.

Every sub-tribe fell under the authority of the ruling sheikh, whose decision was final and whose view preeminent. The chieftain was a one-man government, arbitrating family disputes, declaring war on other tribes, levying taxes on the pearlers, negotiating trade terms, receiving foreign dignitaries, and instilling a sense of loyalty and orthodoxy among his people. He had the power to bring peace and new trade, or foster treachery and bloodshed. Although there was no one above him, and in theory his power was absolute, he was in fact held in check. If he did not listen to his people, and judge matters of tax, war and division of food with prudence and wisdom, he would lose their loyalty to another tribe or master. Thus the sheikhdoms bound themselves into tight, self-serving hierarchies, in which everyone's needs were considered. Down the centuries there was never any need to change this mutually satisfying framework of governance.

FORTY YEARS AGO, driving out into the Liwa felt like passing over the edge of the known world. One would eat around a campfire, and sleep under the speckled canopy of stars. In the cold, dewy mornings one would shake out shoes for scorpions. Occasionally one would wake to find sleeping bags alive with wriggling desert mice that had come seeking warmth.

Rising over a large crest, Mezaira'a appears as if from nowhere – the heart of the string of settlements that make up the Liwa. It nestles in the dip of a massive rise of sand. There are stoplights, junctions and a huge marble slab that is the Abu Dhabi Islamic Bank. Older style dwellings made of mud-brick flank the new town. There is a dilapidated strip mall, general store, a KFC, dark expanses of lush greenery and strips of sand for boys to kick around in, schools and municipal buildings. The town appears cupped in some giant hidden hand. But what was remote until then – there was no asphalt road until 1978 – is now a pit-stop town of about 30,000.

Beyond there is only the sand, a shimmering, empty wilderness. The beginning of the Rub' al Khali, the Empty Quarter, almost a million square miles of sand billowing like a great golden blanket as far as the eye can see. There was no escape out there. The bedu, those dwellers on open land, live side by side with their expansive, omnipresent god, privileged enough simply to be. As one sinks barefoot into the slopes, it is impossible to pretend we are significant. The desert eases time and geography into one. It has stayed as it was – one of the last great uninhabited spaces of the world.

The Bani Yas, like their kin in Dubai, but not the other five northern emirates' ruling families, are southern Arabs. The Bani Yas migrated to the shores of the Gulf sometime before the 1600s, coming primarily from the Najd, the central province of modern Saudi Arabia. Even further back they hailed from the Wadi Nahyan near Marib in Yemen.

The earliest recorded reference to the Bani Yas indicates they were in or near Abu Dhabi as early as the beginning of the 1600s. It is certain that the most recent tribal homeland of the Bani Yas was the Liwa. They shared the oases with one other tribe, the Manasir, who had arrived at perhaps the same time. The two tribes became steadfast allies. The Bani Yas tended their date palms and grazed their herds in the deserts around Liwa, while some sections migrated to the coast on a seasonal basis for fishing and pearling.

Sometime in the late 1600s or early 1700s, the Al Bu Falah section, which was and remains one of the smallest sections of the Bani Yas, emerged as the section which gave the tribe its ruling family – the Al-Nahyan. Nahyan himself was the son of a leading sheikh of the Bani Yas circa 1700 named Falah. Falah was either the son or perhaps the grandson of the putative, eponymic founder of the Bani Yas.

In 1762 the Al Bu Falah family discovered Abu Dhabi Island. A group of huntsmen had been sent by their chieftain, Sheikh Dhiyab bin Issa, in search of food for the tribe. Following tracks they spotted a single gazelle over a golden dune and began to stalk her, following her through dusk into the night, and on into the next day. It was the start of a long journey that drew them north, to where the golden sands and scrub yielded to glistening white salt flats and the translucent coral water of the Gulf. By the sea, they lost the gazelle when a thick coastal mist blew in and obscured her from view. The hunters were ready to turn back when the mist began to burn off and they spied her again – across the water, her silhouette clear enough for them to follow.

With their robes and scarves trailing in the shallows, they crossed the causeway to the island. After scrambling over breeze blown ridges they reached the spot where the gazelle had been and found a spring trickling up from beneath the scrub. It was water, brackish but fresh. When the tribesmen returned with the news, Dhiyab bin Issa named the island Abu Dhabi, "Father of the Gazelle." The Al Bu Falah returned to protect their find, and in 1793 they made the island their permanent home. They built an imposing coral stone fort, the Qasr al-Hosn, close to the spring. Today's ruling family is directly descended from those first settlers.

A succeeding ruler, Shakhbut bin Dhiyab, established the Bani Yas' interest in another new settled area, the oasis of Buraimi and Al-Ain. By the 1820s they would have outright ownership of some of the Buraimi settlements and by the 1850s they were firmly established as important landowners in the area, displacing to some degree the previous tribal powers, the Naim and the Dhawahir.

As the nineteenth century progressed, the Al-Nahyan and the Bani Yas became the most powerful tribe in the area, which extended from Liwa in the south to Abu Dhabi Island in the north, and from the Bani Yas' camel herding dar at Khor al-Udeid in the west to Buraimi in the east – roughly the boundaries of modern Abu Dhabi. Their story had only just begun

DAGGERS

ARABIA IS A LAND of terrible heat. A tract of desert the size of Western Europe, practically untouched by the world until the 1940s. To anybody who doesn't live there, it seems a land of mystery and romance. Some still think of it as a land of exotic promises – of harems and Arabian nights. In reality, it is a harsh and lonely place. Only water makes Arabia bearable and where there is water there is life. Water is so important that the Arabian oasis became the inspiration for the Muslim idea of heaven.

When you come to the cool shade of the date gardens after the heat and emptiness of the desert, the oasis seems literally heaven – a place of pure pleasure. Every well in the desert is like a port. The camel caravans crossed the desert like ships cross the sea. There were no frontiers, no fixed territories, and no land belonging to anyone.

There were just the wondering bedouin and their camels, attached to each other like sailors to their ships, bringing their trade to the desert markets. It was a hard life in Arabia and it bred hard men, but its inhabitants were as perfectly adjusted to the hard land as they were in the days of Abraham, the father of all the tribes.

The Bani Yas had long been considered a fierce rival of the Qawasim tribal confederation, the other important tribal grouping in the region. The Qawasim opposed the British fleet, so in 1820 the Government of India in

Bombay mounted an overwhelming attack on their headquarters at Sharjah and Ras Al-Khaimah, in order to support British allies in the region and to protect its interests in the Gulf and the Indian Ocean. The defeat of the Qawasim, and an agreement the British called the "General Treaty for the Cessation of Plunder and Piracy by Land and Sea," signed in 1820, ushered in an era of relative maritime tranquility. That accord was followed by the "Perpetual Maritime Truce" agreement in 1853, after which the term 'Pirate Coast" was supplanted by "Trucial Coast." The sheikhdoms whose rulers had signed the 1853 agreement became known as the 'Trucial States', an epithet that survived until 1971 when they were all united under the banner of the newly created federation, the United Arab Emirates.

These two agreements formed the foundation of British relations with the coastal sheikhdoms. The British authorities undertook to protect them from all aggression. In return, their foreign relations were conducted through the British government, which excluded all other powers from direct contact with any of them. Among these statelets was Abu Dhabi, whose ruler signed an Exclusive Agreement with Britain in 1892, in which he pledged not to "cede, sell, mortgage or otherwise give for occupation any part of [his] territory, save to the British Government" in return for British protection.

Once the power of the Qawasim had been curtailed, that of the Bani Yas – a land power – began to grow correspondingly. It reached its peak during the rule of Sheikh Zayed bin Khalifa of Abu Dhabi. Known as Zayed the Great, he ruled from 1855-1909 and related himself by marriage to numerous tribes of the Oman coast and the interior, thereby extending his authority over many of the neighboring tribes. By the end of the nineteenth century the town of Abu Dhabi, the hub of the sheikhdom, had an estimated population of 6,000, and fourth-fifths of the ruler's income annual income of about $75,500 was derived from dues on pearl boats and other income dependent on the pearl industry.

Zayed the Great's death in 1909 marked the end of Abu Dhabi's dominance of the Trucial Coast. Without an established order of succession, Abu Dhabi went through a long period of instability. Zayed had married a large number of wives, such alliances cementing the loyalty of the various sections of the Bani Yas and other tribes and allowing for a long period of stability in Abu Dhabi during the nineteenth century. He also sired a large number of sons – most being only half brothers who had grown up in separate households – and this led to a dynastic crisis following his death.

Khalifa, the eldest of Sheikh Zayed's seven sons, was the obvious candidate to take over. His mother and wife were both of the Manasir tribe, the Al-Nahyan's oldest allies, and he had strong tribal support. That he had founded new settlements at Buraimi gave him more legitimacy. Yet Khalifa, perhaps because his mother and wife feared for his safety, refused to occupy the ruler's fort. Such fears were well-grounded. Except for Khalifa's father, every ruler of Abu Dhabi since Issa bin Nahyan in the eighteenth century had either been killed or overthrown.

Instead, the late leader was succeeded by his second son, Sheikh Tahnoon bin Zayed (1909-1912). Tahnoon proved to be an incompetent ruler and died of ill health just a few years into his reign. The elders of the Bani Yas again approached Khalifa and again he refused the succession. Another younger brother, Hamdan bin Zayed (1912-1922), became ruler. Hamdan was unable to quell tribal fighting in the southern and western regions of the emirate. Then pearling entered a state of decline after the First World War and Hamdan was forced to raise taxes, earning the resentment of Abu Dhabi's merchants. Many of his subjects left the sheikhdom, and although he visited them and convinced them to return, they remained discontented. When he suspended the subsidies usually paid to members of the ruling family and their key allies, he came under heavy criticism from his younger brothers.

In 1922 Sultan bin Zayed, the most powerful of the younger brothers, murdered Hamdan with the direct assistance of a half-brother, Saqr, and seized control of the ruler's fort. It seems the conspirators were egged on by acquisitive wives and were disappointed to find Hamdan's treasury nearly empty. Despite the atrocity, Sultan had support among the people and the reluctant backing of his eldest brother Khalifa.

THE MODERN STORY of the House of Nahyan began in about 1904 when Sultan bin Zayed, then about 24-years old, married the 13-year old Salaama bint Butti Al-Qubaisi. She was from Mezaira'a in the Liwa. The marriage – she remained Sultan's only wife – went a long way toward strengthening relations between the Nahyan and the Qubaisat, a tribe which had left Abu Dhabi several times in the nineteenth century. Salaama bore four sons: Shakhbut (1904) Haza'a (1905) Khaled (1906) and Zayed (*c.* 1910).

After killing his brother Hamdan, in 1922 the 41-year old Sultan became ruler of Abu Dhabi. Before long he too was in an impossible situation. The region-wide pearling recession was intensifying and he had no way of raising the revenues needed to restore former subsidies. He soon aroused the tribes' growing dissatisfaction and began to face opposition within the family.

In late July 1926 Sultan sent his wife and several children of his children to Buraimi, where the summers were not so harsh. The pearling trade had remained in a deepening recession and Sultan, with an empty treasury, was quickly losing support. At a family dinner on August 4, Sultan was shot in the back and killed by half-brother Saqr bin Zayed (1926-1928). His son Khaled was wounded in the ambush but managed to escape. Salaama and her other sons took refuge with the governor of Buraimi until, at the urging of her husband's brother Khalifa, she left for Sharjah.

Disgusted by his younger siblings, Khalifa re-entered politics and organized a secret pact against the disreputable Saqr, who had meanwhile invited foreign interference in Abu Dhabi's affairs by offering tributes to the hated Saudi Wahabis in return for support.

Soon the new ruler of Abu Dhabi became entangled in a deteriorating dispute with the Manasir, the nomadic tribe of the Dhafrah region in the interior. While plotting to kill his elder brother Khalifa (who had managed to come to terms with the Manasir), Sheikh Saqr was himself executed by a group of Manasir tribesmen – agents of Khalifa – in early 1928. Khalifa accepted responsibility for the latest murder, banished Saqr's children from Abu Dhabi, and restored Sultan's bloodline.

The role of ruler now fell on the eldest son of Sultan, the 25-year-old Shakhbut. That year the influential Salaama brought her sons together and made them swear a solemn oath to never resort to fratricide. It was a decisive break from the past. The path towards stability had been paved.

Sheikh Shakhbut bin Sultan remained in power for nearly forty years. Ascending the throne after a period of almost constant political turmoil, he inherited a deteriorating political situation. It was not surprising that British officials were of the opinion that the new sheikh would rule for a considerably shorter period than the eighteen months of his predecessor. Even worse, he soon had to face an economic threat as well: forces beyond the control of Abu Dhabi were to deprive it of its last source of vitality – pearl fishing.

The early part of the twentieth century was a period of relative boom for Persian Gulf pearls, and quite naturally Abu Dhabi benefited. Although the bulk of the pearls found their way to Bahrain for distribution to India and Europe, a large portion of the pearling fleet was supplied by the Trucial Coast, and in particular by Abu Dhabi.

During the reign of Zayed the Great, Abu Dhabi had steadily increased its participation in pearling, which meant an increased income not only for those directly dependent upon the trade but also for those who benefited from the flow of wealth it brought into the emirate. Abu Dhabi was almost exclusively reliant on its pearling income in an area that had little else to offer. Without this revenue, the economy of Abu Dhabi would rapidly decline. Indeed, this happened soon after the beginning of Sheikh Shakhbut's reign. The Gulf pearling industry was effectively destroyed by the worldwide depression of the late 1920s and early 1930s, and by the introduction of the much cheaper Japanese cultured pearl.

The economic and social conditions of the chiefdom were rudimentary. There was virtually none of the infrastructure normally regarded as necessary – roads, motorized transport, hospitals, electricity, etc. The political system in Abu Dhabi was, by Western criteria, equally rudimentary if not anarchic, but not without its own logic. With nearly the entire population being organized along tribal lines and adhering to tribal values and customs, the most important political factor was that allegiance and loyalty were offered on a personal basis. Hence the European concepts of the nation-state and of territorial sovereignty were neither applicable nor comprehensible. Tribal politics was concerned with authority over people, not territory: The political unit was not a territorial concept but was people-centered. Further the ruler – or tribal leader – had to earn allegiance and poor performance was critically assessed.

Lack of *baraka* (blessing), a period of ill luck, or a major quarrel could drastically reduce the number of followers and, through them, the territorial holdings deemed to be within the sphere of influence of the ruler or sheikh in question. Thus, whereas the territory of a state was defined in terms of established tribal allegiances and tribal territory, the political institutions of Abu Dhabi were based on personal and tribal loyalties. Allegiances were, therefore, extremely fluid, because inter-state rivalry was essentially tribal. Yet it was not a place of anarchy in the strict sense because conflict was a functional part of the total system.

A most instructive illustration of this was the secession of the Al Bu Falasa section of the Bani Yas in the 1830s, during the rule of the fourth sheikh, Khalifa bin Shakhbut (1833-1845). Dissatisfied with his rule, the Al Bu Falasa migrated and established a new settlement at Dubai, which has been a politically separate center ever since.

The main population centers within Abu Dhabi were the town itself and the oases of Buraimi and Liwa. In addition, there were semi-nomads living on a few islands and nomads who roamed the Dhafrah region, the northern part of the Rub' al-Khali basin. In the sheikhdom of Abu Dhabi, the balance between townspeople and nomads occurred naturally. Those settled along the coasts provided dried fish, goods and services, while the inhabitants of the oases supplied dates and vegetables. The nomads moved among the settled areas and provided meat and other animal products. It was a comfortable balance.

Not surprisingly, observers such as Major Clarence Mann noted: "Except for some Persian shopkeepers in Abu Dhabi town and Buraimi, it was a homogeneous population based on tribal patterns."

Although young and inexperienced, Shakhbut ruled the sheikhdom to the satisfaction of the tribal chiefs. His correct and affable manner helped him maintain friendly and conciliatory relations. Above all, he knew how to deal with tribal leaders by exercising minimal control and leaving internal affairs to them.

MILLIONS OF YEARS ago the Arabian Plate drifted slowly out of the southern hemisphere until it collided with Eurasia. After leaving ranges of mountains from Oman to Iran, the Arabian Plate tilted and its eastern flank was forced downwards to become part of the Tethys Sea, the warm, shallow waters rich in plankton and other organics. The essential components of what would one day be petroleum. There the great oil fields were formed and the destiny of Abu Dhabi was determined.

Hundreds of thousands of lifetimes later, in the 1930s, Abu Dhabi was one of the poorest areas in the world. In the 1930s, after the decline of the pearl trade, many in Abu Dhabi were so poor they were forced to eat raw food since they could not afford wood to make fires.

Sheikh Shakhbut was not looking for miracles. In his parched domains, he was simply seeking a better water supply and readily agreed to a proposal for British geologists to undertake a survey. Then he heard what the oil companies were paying his fellow sheikhs for prospecting rights. Exploration began in 1936 when a subsidiary of Iraq Petroleum Company (IPC) was sent to Abu Dhabi to search for onshore fields. They proceeded slowly inland accompanied by the sheikh so as not to alarm the locals with their presence. That first survey covered all the way from Abu Dhabi Island to Al-Ain and Jebel Hafit but brought only violent thunderstorms and exaggeration. Still Shakhbut agreed for the efforts to continue and IPC, through the subsidiary company, Petroleum Development (Trucial Coast) Limited (PDTC) obtained a concession agreement with Abu Dhabi in 1939.

No oil was found and for the next decade little changed in the sheikhdom. Shakhbut and his family relied on payments from the oil company and scanty income from their date gardens around Al-Ain. New seismic techniques that could identify the underlying rock structures were soon employed by survey parties roaming the hinterland and PDTC began drilling for oil at Ras Sadr in 1950. Soon exploration began offshore.

As the expectation of finding oil increased, garish stories were emerging out of Saudi Arabia. Vulgar extravagance and materialism were fundamentally at odds with the minimalism of bedouin life. Shakhbut was actually quite curious about the modern world but his natural caution and conservatism took over. He was determined to protect his people and their way of life.

This was not a problem, as long oil remained a pipe dream. At Shakhbut's *majlis* in the fort on Abu Dhabi Island, with guards and tribesmen flanking the room, he was philosophical. It had been 19 years since the first survey for oil.

"We have waited a long time for news of oil in Abu Dhabi," Shakhbut told a visitor. "It is a long time to wait."

His brother Khaled nodded and echoed the sentiment.

"A long time to wait."

Shakhbut was silent for a moment.

"It is the will of Allah," he said.

The old rhythm of life held and they did not know then what the future held in store. Oil would bring a revolution, ending centuries of Arabian isolation, and sweep Shakhbut away. The old, simple life of Arabia, the only life they knew, would be cracked wide open.

BROTHERS

A HUNDRED YEARS AGO Liwa was all but unknown to Europeans. A collection of about three dozen bedouin settlements gathered around the water wells and groves of date palms among the dunes. Most of the inhabitants were from the Bani Yas federation and the Manasir tribe, the old tribes who peopled the desert in winter and the coast in summer. The earliest permanent structures in Liwa, dating to the early 19th century, were forts from which the Bani Yas protected their oases. They were Maliki Sunnis who often fought the strict Wahabis from the lands of the House of Saud to the west.

Zayed bin Sultan, the youngest of the four sons of Sultan bin Zayed Al-Nahyan and Salaama bint Butti, was born sometime between 1908 and 1912. The date is uncertain and the official date intentionally makes him younger. He was born in Liwa. Like his older brothers, it is likely that Zayed was born in the village of Mujib, where his father had date palm orchards. Nothing can be confirmed with certainty.

The water that bubbled to the surface in Liwa was clear and cool, making the area a haven for people, sheep and camels. There were rabbits and small game to be found. The palms grew tall and the dates were plentiful, the trees providing building materials and everything needed to make ropes and baskets.

As a young boy Zayed had been whisked away to Sharjah following his father's murder during the height of the fratricides of the 1920s. He attended the majlis of his grandfather, Butti bin Khadim Al-Qubaisi, and listened to the debates, usually concerning war or the tribal disputes that dominated those troubled years. In his early childhood he would have learned how to deal with animals, falcons, and weapons, and acquired knowledge of winds, stars and directions. He would have become versed in the oral histories and genealogy of his family. During the autumn Zayed and his brothers hunted deer in the desert, using arrows, spears or daggers.

Zayed grew to manhood around Buraimi, with the sheikhs of the Qubaisat and his maternal grandmother's tribe, the Sultan. The bedu respected him because he was one of them. A tall, powerfully built man with a broad face and straightforward look in his eyes, Zayed knew their legends and songs and rhythmic chants. He rode spirited stallions and could handle a camel as if he had spent his life in the desert. He could also quote as fluently from the Qur'an as from the works of Al Mutanabbi. He was the man who dispensed justice and mediated disputes among the tribes, who oversaw endless consultations over issues in dispute.

A VISITOR TO the Buraimi Oasis in the 1950s would have found the scene entirely out of keeping with what they would have expected. One usually thinks of an oasis being an area of luxurious vegetation surrounded by the desert. Surrounded by the desert it was, but Buraimi stretched for square miles, a collection of villages each with its own well and varying amounts of vegetation. Each village was separated by some miles where the greenery suddenly stopped and you were in sand dunes again. The main street of Al-Ain, the primary village, was like something out of an old west film, broad and dusty. It was only missing a saloon.

The area had been ruled by Sheikh Shakhbut's youngest brother Zayed since 1946. With the death of his old uncle Khalifa bin Zayed at the age of ninety the previous year he was effectively the ruler's deputy.

The village of Muwaij'ei is situated on the extreme west of the Buraimi Oasis. It was a patch of productive land and vast date palm plantations owned by the Al-Nahyan. Old Khalifa bin Zayed had established a settlement there, as it was within the agricultural estates he had acquired in the area. Muwaij'ei had a beautiful atmosphere, plentiful water and its palm trees, which provided building materials and dates, a rich source of energy.

When Zayed became his brother's deputy in Al-Ain, he made Muwaij'ei his residence. The imposing fort there had been built in the 1920s by Khalifa bin Zayed. Situated on flat terrain outside the palm orchards, this square edifice was constructed of mud, stone and palm trunks and surrounded by walls, with towers at three of the four angles.

Yet Zayed was a busy man and usually difficult to find. He had a number of residences in the area and it could be a major occupation finding where he was residing at any given time. A visitor could easily spend all morning, if not all day, being directed from one to another until he finally tracked Zayed down. He was then always entertained to coffee and candied fruit and nuts or sometimes even to dinner.

Buraimi was an important place. Key to the emirates' hinterland it had strategic as well as economic importance, providing the bulk of Abu Dhabi's agricultural products. It was an attractive prize and there were determined poachers in the neighborhood with long memories. Zayed's tenure as governor witnessed the so-called Buraimi dispute, where the Saudi kingdom, flush with money and ambition, tried to bully its tiny neighbor out of existence.

The struggle between the Al-Saud and Al-Nahyan dynasties can be traced to 1810 when the Al-Saud, already in control of most of eastern Arabia, took control of the Buraimi Oasis, the traditional territory of the Al-Nahyan, at the time poor herdsman and pearl fishermen. The Al-Saud brought with them a puritanical form of Islam – Wahabism – which to this day Emirati leaders complain about as responsible for extremism and intolerance in the region. For 150 years control of the Buraimi Oasis fell in and out of Al-Saud control. They occupied the oasis five times between 1800 and 1869.

In 1952, a small Saudi force led by Turki bin Abdullah al-Otaishan occupied the village of Hamasa in the Buraimi Oasis (the so-called Buraimi dispute). Zayed prominently and staunchly opposed the Saudis territorial claims and reportedly rejected a bribe of about £30 million to allow ARAMCO to explore for oil in the disputed territory. As part of this dispute, Zayed and his brother Haza'a attended the Buraimi arbitration tribunal in Geneva in September 1955 and gave evidence to its members. When the tribunal was abandoned amid allegations of Saudi bribery, the British initiated the reoccupation of the oasis. In 1955 the Saudis were expelled by force by Abu Dhabi and Omani troops

The affair helped to establish Zayed's legendary reputation, the man who succeeded in repulsing the oil-rich Saudis and their American cronies long before Abu Dhabi had found its own huge oil reserves. As one foreign observer put it, "[Zayed] was very proud that, when he had nothing, he told them to get stuffed."

The British had already begun to view him as a successor to Shakhbut. One glowing British report of 1952 described Zayed as universally popular, saying that he was "respected, almost revered as a man, the only real man among the four brothers, a man of physical and mental strength used to taking big and bold decisions, a fine organizer and a clean liver."

WATER HAD A UNIQUE hold on the bedouin mind and is close to their spirit. Some wells were salty, others harsh and bitter, some sulfurous, and others sweet as rainwater. Water had a powerful effect, for it determined the rise and fall of settlements and trade routes. It instilled in the Arab mind a love of greenery and streams and most of all of the oases. There was a strong fascination about finding water beneath a bleak and desiccated land.

Shakhbut's early interest was drilling for water, not oil. Zayed's passion was also water.

The people of Buraimi owed their existence to the *aflaj*. They were to the sheikhdom what the aqueducts were to ancient Rome. Both a feat of unschooled engineering and a vital link in the irrigation system, these underground conduits brought water run off to the fields from the mountains of Jebel Hafit. Without these literal lifelines, green patches of land like Muwaij'ei would have reverted to barren desert.

For some years the area existed in a vacuum of political authority and the conduits had fallen into disrepair. In 1948 Zayed set the men of the oasis to dredging, cleaning and restoring damaged and neglected channels. He also constructed a major new watercourse and provided water pumps to farmers willing to cultivate new areas. These efforts had a notable effect.

In Muwaij'ei in 1955 the palm grove could be watered once every five weeks. In October of that year over a third could not be watered at all and the trees were dying. By 1960 the entire grove could be watered about every three weeks. In time the area was flourishing with palms, lemons, figs and grapes.

Zayed's policies as governor reflected an animus fundamentally bedouin in nature that was anti-wealth, whether that of merchants or landowners. He confronted prosperous farmers who had cornered most of the water distribution rights, thereby denying adequate irrigation for many small landowners. They refused Zayed's request to provide the latter with free water. Zayed prevailed by providing free water from the Al-Nahyan's holdings and denied the wealthy landowners access to the newly constructed water channel.

Soon the plantations of the Buraimi were irrigated and fertile. Zayed's improvements were so great that the flow of water trebled and agricultural output increased enormously.

Apart from his particular interest in the restoration of the falaj system, Zayed did whatever he could to encourage development in the region. His projects were entirely dependent on Shakhbut financing them and getting anything approved involved frustration and complications.

Trade flourished in Al-Ain. Zayed helped in the building of small shops and allowed merchants to trade in the souks without paying rent. But his greatest achievement came in social development. In Muwaij'ei Zayed established a court of justice and built a small school and employed Jordanian teachers. In 1960 American missionary doctors set up a clinic which became the Oasis Hospital in 1963 (far ahead Abu Dhabi at the time). Such facilities were hitherto unknown in Abu Dhabi. Many townsfolk could not afford consultations or medications so Zayed would issue them a permission slip that bore the stamp of his own signet ring. On the production of this document, they would receive treatment and then Zayed would foot the hospital bills himself.

Zayed's popular and effective authority quickly reestablished the loyalty of the tribes of the interior to Abu Dhabi and his family's hold on Al-Ain. The bedouin began to settle there and the population steadily increased.

1958 WAS A PIVOTAL year in the history of Abu Dhabi and in the life of Zayed. Two events shaped what was to come. Oil was discovered off the coast in 1958 and Zayed's brother Haza'a died of cancer. The other brother, Khaled, whom people called "cold coffee," was generally disliked. One report said that Khaled had never recovered from witnessing his father's murder and remained high strung and nervous for the rest of his life.

Previously Zayed had shown few signs of political ambition, only marrying sporadically. He married his cousin Hussa bint Mohammed Al-Nahyan in 1936. She suffered numerous miscarriages before bearing his son, Khalifa, in 1946 or 1948. Another marriage, to a woman named Fatima, produced a daughter named Salaama. Another wife, from the Mishaghin section of the Bani Yas, gave birth in 1955 to a second son, Sultan.

With Haza'a's death, Zayed was left alone to deal with Shakhbut. He now glimpsed the real prospect of one day ruling the sheikhdom. Zayed proceeded to expand his power base among the tribes of the emirate and extend his influence, particularly in the oasis of Al-Ain. And that meant marriage, the most traditional of practices. In effect, Zayed began to create his own dynasty.

Zayed's marriages accelerated after 1958, with women of the Al Bu Khail, the Bani Qitab, and two from the most prominent subsections of the Dhawahir – a tribe whose relationship with his family had cooled during the conflict of the 1950s. Historically, the Dhawahir were the other major tribal pillar of support for the Al-Nahyan, second only to the Manasir.

Those four marriages – to Moza bint Suhail Al-Khaili, Fatima bint Mubarak Al-Kitbi, Aisha bint Ali Al-Darmaki and Amna bint Salah Al-Badi – made between 1959 and 1965, produced 27 of his 30 children.

Fatima bore six sons – Mohammed (1961), Hamdan (1963), Haza'a (1965), Tahnoon (1969), Mansour (1970), Abdullah (1972) – and two daughters – Shamma (1967) and Alyazia (1968).

Moza bore five sons – Saif (1968), Ahmed (1969), Hamed (1971), Omar (1972), Khaled (1978) and two daughters – Shamsa (1960) and Afra (1966).

Aisha added four more sons and five daughters – Saeed (1965), Nahyan (1967), Falah (1970), Dhiyab (1971), Latifa (1963), Moza (1964), Wadima (1969), Sheikha (1974), and Maitha (1976).

Amna gave birth to two sons and a daughter – Issa (1966), Nasser (1968), and Roda (1970). As may have been expected, Zayed's matrimonial activities were "a source much merriment among the bedu, who are delighted that he makes up for the poor achievements of his brothers in this direction."

FAR FROM THE comparative "civilization" of Buraimi, Abu Dhabi town remained a stagnant and desultory settlement of a few thousand. They lived in *barasti* huts or small houses built of mud and strengthened with coral. From his palace in Abu Dhabi, the Al-Hosn, an old fort surrounded by a few scattered palms, Shakhbut had ruled Abu Dhabi for more than thirty years in poverty and comparative peace. Shakhbut's rule was traditional. His word was law, but he remained close to his subjects. Anyone was free to talk to him any day in the majlis. And as long as the people had no money they were all relatively contented. He had become ruler following twenty years of political instability marked by tribal fighting in the western and southern areas of the sheikhdom. In his years as ruler, Shakhbut managed to reestablish stability and reassert his authority over the tribes.

Abu Dhabi was a poor pastoral, agriculture and fishing society. Then in the 1960s the sheikhdom struck it rich and its troubles started. Revenue increased enormously when commercial drilling and exports started in earnest in 1962. In a year or two people were demonstrating about work or wages after having neither in their lives before. By the end of the decade, Abu Dhabi would be awash with more money than its inhabitants could fathom.

The grumbles grew as the money mounted because Shakhbut was a miser. All his life he had been a poor man and when he became rich the skinflint habits stuck. He found his money made few friends. His poverty-stricken state was on the verge of unbelievable wealth but Shakhbut refused to allow economic development. A ruler who was unmoved by all the talk of progress, he was unable or unwilling to realize how radically the circumstances had changed. Why did his people need hospitals or schools when they had survived without such things in the past?

Shakhbut came to power just before the Great Depression and had witnessed the hard times that had followed the collapse of the pearling trade. These formative experiences deeply shaped his world view. Hugh Boustead, the British Political Agent in Abu Dhabi, reported that "it is clearly no easy task for a Ruler, after a lifetime of poverty, to accustom himself to the idea that his income will henceforward be counted not in the hundreds of pounds but in millions."

While the old generation of British Arabists often waxed poetic over the pristine desert, the natives knew only a harsh, often deadly place. They could not romanticize a difficult life, where starvation was not uncommon. Oil money had led to material progress elsewhere on the coast and the Bahrainis and Qataris had air-conditioning and shoes in the late-1950s. The Emiratis were quite aware of such happenings and it was not long before they began to view the past as an embarrassment, evidence of their ancient poverty, struggles and insignificance. They knew what they lacked and when the oil money came began to despise what they did not have.

The people began to say that Zayed would be a better ruler; he had a mind more open to the world, he was generous, he was a man's man. But Zayed showed an extraordinary amount of loyalty to his elder brother. In 1954 when Shakhbut threatened to resign after reducing the allowances of his relatives, Zayed and his brothers begged him to reconsider. Such was the power of the oath Salaama bint Butti extracted from her sons in 1928. True to his promise, Zayed would never harm Shakhbut.

But Zayed was growing displeased with his brother and chafed under his rule. Zayed was not a rich man and his projects depended on a meager income provided by his brother. That allowance was not enough to cover the costs of governing Buraimi and Zayed supplemented his income with gifts from his mother and uncle.

During the second half of 1962 there was some evidence of development in Abu Dhabi: two British engineering firms jointly submitted a development plan and some unpaved roads were constructed. When Shakhbut was shown a masterplan for a new city he purportedly said "...this is Paris! We don't want a Paris in Abu Dhabi." The ruler had already imposed a ban on any new construction.

Shakhbut was adamant about preserving a traditional lifestyle. He refused to generate electricity, with the exception of the palace, which ran on portable generators. What rankled Abu Dhabians the most was how Shakhbut spent lavishly on his two profligate, alcoholic sons.

Shakhbut's decisions remained absolute; he refused to listen to advice or to tolerate family pressure, and his brothers realized that nothing could change his mind. It is hardly surprising that when he invited them to carry out the changes, his brothers were hesitant to accept. Perhaps they suspected that Shakhbut intended to let them accept responsibility, without real power to carry out the proposed reforms. Specifically, Shakhbut suspected that his brother Zayed was behind the drive to influence him. When some of his relatives came to talk to him, almost pleading, he warned them against Zayed's intrigues.

The oil flowed, the money continued to pour in, but Shakhbut would not spend it. He was paralyzed by habit, suspicion and fear. He knew the harsh old world of Arabia but could not meet the challenge of the rich new one.

UNLIKE HIS BROTHER, Zayed was receptive to progress and despaired of his brother's conservatism. Whereas Shakhbut was often unstable and moody, Zayed was "a man of friendly disposition" and a "true Arab gentleman." For the British, Zayed was a man with whom they could do business. And Zayed's loyalty, like his patience, was not inexhaustible.

In the early 1960s British diplomats in the Gulf paid frequent calls on Zayed in Buraimi to discuss the state of affairs in Abu Dhabi. Zayed made no effort to defend his brother's actions and was openly critical of Shakhbut's character and style of government. He warned the British that Shakhbut would never implement a development program. Zayed was well aware of widespread discontent in the sheikhdom and was convinced that his brother was in complete denial and would not change. Shakhbut was only concerned with his own position, with keeping things in Abu Dhabi as much as possible in his own hands. Zayed went as far to question his brother sanity, saying that "he was more convinced than ever that Shakhbut [was] basically mad."

Thus began Zayed's quiet campaign to privately undermine his brother. In his conversations with the British in the early sixties, Zayed was careful to present himself as Shakhbut's opposite – both in political views and character. If he were ruler he would use the oil money for development and build a modern administration. If he were ruler Abu Dhabi would become the "flower of the Gulf."

In May 1963 Zayed made a secret agreement with the British to depose Shakhbut. The optics were key: The British could not afford to look like an imperialist power imposing its will. Zayed could not look like their stooge. The removal of Shakhbut would be presented as an affair of the House of Nahyan. A British messenger would inform the ruler of the "family" decision. The British would then remove Shakhbut from the sheikhdom. The plan fell apart shortly before it was to have taken place. Zayed was "not prepared to go it alone" and could not obtain the support of his brother, Khaled, or senior cousin Mohammed bin Khalifa. They were "weak and ineffective characters," critical of Shakhbut but also afraid of him. At the last minute, Khaled changed his mind, likely after taking a bribe from Shakhbut.

During the following year, Zayed assured the British that he was ready to depose Shakhbut at any time – even offering a written statement – but was not able to rely on the assistance of his family. He could act only with active British help, having "no force of his own with which to overcome Shakhbut's police and bodyguards or to compel him to leave the country."

While many in the Foreign Office believed more than ever that removing Shakhbut was necessary in order to modernize the Persian Gulf, consensus was hard to come by in London. The risks of such a move still seem to outweigh the benefits. Zayed tried to persuade Shakhbut to change his ways. At a meeting in June 1964 Zayed warned him that the ruling family was becoming increasingly unpopular with the people.

"Why?" Shakhbut asked.

"Do you think they do not know that Issa of Bahrain and Rashid of Dubai, who has no oil, are building houses free for the people, so many each year, and are busy putting up schools and dispensaries? What have we done for them? Nothing."

"I know we are popular and I know they like me," Shakhbut said.

Following that discussion, Zayed told Boustead that his brother was in complete denial and that attempts to warn him of the dangers were futile. Zayed's thoughts were already wandering far into the future.

When Zayed visited Abu Dhabi town he liked to examine the goods at Mohan Jashanmal's new department store.

"Jashanmal, show me the films," Zayed would say.

"The ones with girls?" the merchant would joke.

"Show me the films of the tall buildings!" Zayed demanded.

The merchant would hand Zayed a red child's 3D viewer and the sheikh would thumb through slides of New York or English gardens.

"One day you will see," Zayed would say, "The gardens will be here. The tall buildings will be here."

"If you say so," Jashanmal would answer, "But it is very difficult to believe."

BY JULY 1966, almost four years after the first oil shipment had left Abu Dhabi, there was no evidence of real progress in administrative and economic development. Shakhbut had managed to cancel, postpone or obstruct almost every development project submitted to him by his consultants. In April 1966, for instance, he canceled a planned electrification project, and firms who had participated in tenders for this project in Abu Dhabi and Buraimi were disappointed to learn that the ruler had decided not to award a contract at all. One British MP Christopher Tugendhat, who visited Abu Dhabi in May 1966, summed up his impressions:

I found it hard to believe. The airfield is just a strip of tarmac. There are no roads in the capital and the streets are still unpaved. Many inhabitants live in enclosures made of rushes called barasti. All the oil revenues of millions of pounds go personally to the ruler. One day this will create a great storm in this Emirate, if the attitude of the ruler remains that of status quo.

Under pressure from his family, as well as from the British Political Agent, Shakhbut agreed in April 1966 to an outline plan for the government of Abu Dhabi, and following a major row within the ruling family in May he appointed Zayed as president of the Finance Department, although with rather vague powers. At the end of that month he even drew up a civil list, which for the first time fixed the amounts of money to be paid to members of the ruling family. The family was not, however, satisfied with these tokens of progress. Meanwhile, Shakhbut's frequent outbursts of rage were a source of growing concern to senior members of the family.

By then the Al-Nahyan family had the courage to request British intervention. Zayed visited Britain in June or July 1966. It was then the deal was concluded. In a meeting at the Foreign Office, Zayed "asked for an assurance" that if the family deposed Shakhbut the British "would accept him as ruler... and provide him with assistance in the form of an aircraft to take Shakhbut away... This assurance was subsequently given to him."

Thus, after his return, Zayed tried to persuade his brother to step down in an honorable way without the use of force, but to no avail. Considering it an affront, Shakhbut rejected the offer and stated that he would never abdicate. On August 4, a letter deposing the ruler signed by senior members of the family was presented to Hugh Balfour-Paul, the Acting Political Agent in Abu Dhabi. Balfour-Paul personally conveyed the message to Sheikh Shakhbut on August 6. When the ruler boldly turned it down, it was decided to use force as a last resort.

Most sources are vague or silent on the exact details of Shakhbut's removal. It is known, though, that a contingent of soldiers, led by Colonel Edward "Tug" Wilson – whom Zayed stayed with for the two days before the transfer of power – took over the local radio station and surrounded the Al-Hosn Palace with a detachment of soldiers.

The siege lasted almost five hours, but Shakhbut refused to surrender. A handful of soldiers were then ordered to enter the palace and force him to leave. A car, waiting at the front door, carried him to the airport where a special plane was ready to take him to Bahrain and then Beirut. At the same time, Zayed's supporters and well-wishers immediately came to offer congratulations and acknowledge him as the new ruler.

Their mother Sheikha Salaama, in her seventies and crippled with arthritis, was kept in the dark. She was told that Shakhbut had gone away for eye treatment, as it had been forbidden to tell her the truth. A female member of the ruling family was prevented from entering Sheikha Salaama's house to keep her informed of what had happened.

Four years later Zayed allowed Shakhbut to return to live in Al-Ain as long as he stayed out of politics. Zayed and Shakhbut met rarely until 1978 when they both attended their mother's funeral. Afterwards, they saw each other occasionally until Shakhbut's own death in 1989.

Later that day, August 6, 1966, Sheikh Zayed bin Sultan Al-Nahyan took over the reins of power in Abu Dhabi. Zayed was now in command, ready to say farewell to the old Arabia. But how was he going to do it? Even with a new ruler the old life still went on, a timeless, patient life dominated by the desert and the unforgiving sun.

HORIZONS

SHEIKH ZAYED NOW RULED a singular little kingdom in southeastern Arabia – Abu Dhabi – some 25,000 people in a stretch of sand and salt flats about half the size of Denmark. According to British observers Zayed's accession was hailed with relief throughout Abu Dhabi, but no "open jubilation." Apparently, many residents of the sheikhdom did not yet comprehend that Sheikh Shakhbut was truly out. The new ruler was concerned: "Although he knows that his position is basically secure, he is afraid of the stray bullet from a hired assassin's or a madman's gun." As a result, Zayed initially remained within his own majlis under tight security and ordered that his nephews, the sons of his deposed predecessor, be barred from returning to Abu Dhabi.

The British were pleased with Zayed's assumption of power. Archie Lamb, Boustead's successor as the political agent, described Zayed as cheerful and generous, a fine horseman, a leader who enjoyed his role as sheikh, "father of his people." He was a handsome man of average, muscular build – about 5' 7" – given to laugh and flash a toothy smile. He had a large brow, fine hooked nose and full brown beard. His face, like his worn hands, suggested use and long exposure to the sun and sand. He was also considered "gallant to European ladies and with a roving eye for all members of the female sex."

Lamb considered Zayed intelligent and reasonable, open to constructive advice from London. Zayed quickly made it clear that he was independent and not under British suzerainty. Lamb suspected Zayed was "too intelligent and too acute an observer of world affairs" expect British forces to remain in the Gulf forever. According to Lamb, the new ruler envisioned himself "as an Arabian, rather than an Arab." Zayed was a "genial and forthcoming personality," with a "genuine determination to make good use of his colossal wealth."

THE REACTIONS OF Abu Dhabi's neighbors were mixed. Sheikh Saqr of Ras Al-Khaimah was delighted that Sheikh Zayed had replaced his brother and visited Abu Dhabi to greet the new ruler. Zayed immediately agreed to join the other Trucial States and order driving on the right. He also agreed to appoint two representatives to participate in the Trucial Council Deliberative Committee. Together in the Abu Dhabi mosque, Zayed and Saqr pledged their friendship. After leaving Abu Dhabi, Saqr urged the rulers of Sharjah, Ajman and Umm al-Qaiwain to visit Zayed.

A British official in Dubai suggested that Saqr's enthusiasm for the Zayed was not solely based on his perception that the new ruler would promote unity: "I find it difficult to believe that Saqr's joy derived solely from Zayed's warm reception. I suspect that he may have been given money. I also suspect that Saqr may see in Zayed a rival to the Ruler of Dubai worth supporting."

Indeed, Zayed had provided £15,000 to Sheikh Saqr. Abu Dhabi's new ruler saw himself as the protector of the poorer sheikhs. In addition to providing funds to Saqr, he told the four other rulers of the northern Trucial States that he was their friend and would assist them. Whenever they wanted money they were instructed to approach him rather than go begging in Bahrain, Qatar, Kuwait or Saudi Arabia. However, he warned that he wanted no publicity and that his generosity was to remain a secret. "Zayed's belief is that money must be made to circulate in the smaller Trucial States to the north of Dubai and that the Rulers themselves must have money in order to behave as rulers towards their people."

Meanwhile, Sheikh Rashid of Dubai was not pleased that Shakhbut had been ousted. The British wanted to assure Rashid that the deposition of Shakhbut did not indicate a change in Britain's policy of "non-interference in the internal affairs of the sheikhdoms." However, Rashid claimed that the removal of Shakhbut indicated that British protection was "valueless." The ruler of Dubai was convinced that Zayed had moved against his brother Shakhbut at the instigation of the British. According to one British official, Sheikh Rashid wished to discredit Sheikh Zayed "in pursuit of his own ambitions in the Trucial States."

On August 17, 1966 Political Resident Balfour-Paul flew from Bahrain to Dubai to meet with Sheikh Rashid who continued to repeat that all Gulf rulers were deeply distressed and claimed that "Britain was finished as a protecting Power, that they should remove their sterling balances from London." Balfour-Paul asserted that there was no reason for alarm, reminding Sheikh Rashid that earlier he had often described the deposed ruler as a "public menace and disgrace," so why now object to Shakhbut's removal? Pressed, Sheikh Rashid explained that he was distressed by the use of the British led Trucial Oman Scouts to interfere in the internal affairs of a sheikhdom, that Sheikh Zayed should have had "the guts to do the job himself." Now every Gulf ruler had to consider that at any moment the British might move against him.

Rashid's complaining was extraordinarily rich given Dubai's recent history. A decade earlier Rashid had conducted affairs of state for his aged father Saeed and in 1955 he faced a challenge from his uncle, Juma bin Maktoum. According to British records, Juma and his sons "bedeviled and obstructed Rashid's administration," "threatened visitors to Rashid's majlis," and "imposed their own system of taxation." After setting up this parallel state, Juma threatened Rashid personally and demanded that his faction take over Dubai. Rashid persuaded the British to force Juma into exile, an operation aided by the Trucial Scouts. Rashid duly assumed the rulership on his father's death in 1958.

Archie Lamb warned Sheikh Zayed that Sheikh Rashid wished to discredit the British government. Zayed appeared unconcerned. He was confident of the support of the rulers of Ajman, and Umm al-Qaiwain, who had both declared that they were under his orders. Insisting that he had no ambition, but to rule well, to aid his less fortunate brothers, and to live in friendship with all of the Gulf states, Zayed promised to be very careful when Rashid arrived for a visit. He planned to greet him as a "beloved brother" and provide a splendid feast in his honor.

But the British remained concerned. Although it appeared likely that Zayed would attempt to prevent Dubai's ruler from obtaining hegemony over the small northern sheikhdoms, "it would be rash to underestimate Rashid's ability to further his own aims (perhaps with Saudi backing)." British officials expressed concern that competition between the rulers of Dubai and Abu Dhabi would retard the task of uniting the seven Trucial States. Soon after deposing his brother, Zayed had contributed £500,000 to the Trucial States Development Fund.

There were very old historical grievances at play. The relationship between Abu Dhabi and Dubai had been characterized by tension since the 1830s. Both ruling families were branches of the Bani Yas and had been allied until the Al Bu Falasa, of which the Maktoum were descended, broke away from the confederation and migrated to the area of modern Dubai. The relationship between the two ruling families remained strained as Abu Dhabi attempted to regain control.

Throughout the nineteenth century, the two competing powers shifted their alliances back and forth, drawing the Qawasim family into their power plays. In the twentieth century, the competition between the two emirates broke out into a series of border wars. After the removal of Shakhbut, the issue of the boundary between Abu Dhabi and Dubai remained. Rashid had proposed that the two sheikhdoms settle the dispute through arbitration and after assuming power Zayed suggested that the two rulers meet to discuss their difficulties. Zayed was prepared to attempt a "brotherly and neighborly solution."

Three months later it appeared that Zayed and Rashid were able to work together. Although they did not arrive at a final decision about their frontiers, they agreed to continue friendly discussions. At the same time, they decided to coordinate internal security work and consider establishing a Trucial State teacher's training college.

Hence by the end of 1966, it appeared that cooperation between the two most powerful Trucial State rulers had been achieved. The Trucial State Council was moving forward without British domination, oil wealth was rapidly increasing and development plans progressing. Clearly, the establishment of the United Arab Emirates was still a vision, not a certainty, but the available British records point to encouraging signs and an increasing commitment on the part of the rulers to overcome their differences and work together for the benefit of all.

RASHID BIN SAEED AL-MAKTOUM had done for Dubai all the things Shakhbut had failed to do for Abu Dhabi. Like the merchant princes of old, the 60-year old Rashid recognized trade as the key to future prosperity. While Shakhbut appeared reluctant to permit change, Rashid encouraged development. If Zayed was the traditional tribal leader, Rashid was more the Levantine entrepreneur.

Rashid's core maxim, one which had sustained his family's rule since 1831, was "What's good for the merchants is good for Dubai." Had Rashid flouted that rule he would most likely be writing his own obituary, as the small group of leading families and Al-Maktoum sheikhs would have found a way to remove him.

In 1957, prior to the discovery of oil, a Dubai Municipal Council had been formed and together with the ruler, began an extensive planning program. Three years later Dubai's creek was dredged and a breakwater built to prevent sand bars forming, allowing larger ships to dock. An airport was opened, a modem telephone system installed, and work on new electrical and water supply facilities was in progress. Meanwhile, smuggling remained an important economic activity in Dubai. Gold was freely imported into the sheikhdom and then "with the connivance of poorly paid" customs officials transported to India and Pakistan in motorized dhows. The word around the Gulf was that Rashid had grown rich smuggling 220 tons of gold a year.

Rashid referred to his city as "the Venice of the East." Unlike the other rulers of the region, Rashid did not receive visitors in the usual majlis, but in a small office furnished with a steel desk where he actively promoted the development of his territory and opportunity for his 45,000 subjects. Diplomats were amazed at Dubai's commercial activity and impressed by the energy and ability of Rashid, who had created a modern town before he had the benefit of oil wealth: "It requires a conscious and continuous effort not to be captivated by Sheikh Rashid's devastating charm, with which goes an agile brain, simplicity of personal life, generosity, and an immense capacity for hard work. One has to remind oneself continually how devious he is and how ruthless he is capable of being when he sees his objective clearly."

Rashid would be Zayed's foil, partner and rival for the next fifteen years.

EVERYTHING BEGAN TO CHANGE. A decade before there was only one plane a week; now there was more than one a day and the place could not quite cope. In Abu Dhabi town there was not much sign of change at first sight. Shakhbut's stagnant rule left the town nearly as squalid as it always had been. Now Zayed was ready to spend his millions.

People had no clue what was about to happen. Five or six years before the people of Abu Dhabi were sunk in the poverty of a thousand years. The twentieth century had passed them by. The alleys were still dark and dirty, the beggars waiting for the faithful to do their duty mandated by the Prophet Mohammed and give them alms. The town of Abu Dhabi, with its 15,000 – 20,000 souls, seemed to explode overnight.

In 1966 it fell to Zayed to bring Abu Dhabi out of the dark ages. For five years after the oil began to flow Abu Dhabi got nothing but piecemeal changes. Zayed came to power with a plan to make Abu Dhabi the model state of

Arabia, with all the paraphernalia of development. In the first few months of his rule, he awarded $70 million worth of contracts and was out every day to spur on the men who were making him a brand new kingdom.

The whole place had a heady atmosphere. The people quickly put their shares of Zayed's inheritance to use. The souk, the bazaar or marketplace, was Abu Dhabi's 5th Avenue and neighborhood supermarket rolled into one. To the desert Arab it was the equivalent of a big city but was not much of a place. Some of the people quickly bought big cars to go bumping over unmade tracks or big lorries to cash in on the building boom and soon learned to throw them away like their fellow modern men.

Zayed had no choice but to be an energized man. He envisioned an ocean boulevard with ribbons of light, flowers and lush palms and his planners set out to make it a reality. Bulldozers began to destroy the old life, houses and such, so a new Arabia could properly be born. The state had to be built from scratch. To create a government he drew up a list of departments, staffed them and ordered offices to be built to house them. Planners were hired to lay out the city in a sensible grid, running power and phone wires, sewer and water lines beneath them. A pair of diesel generators brought power and a desalination plant would be built to distill drinking water from the Gulf. Electricity and telephones arrived in 1967.

Money in the banks meant money to buy things and the beach at Abu Dhabi became piled with purchases. Abu Dhabi was built on a sandbank and had never had a proper harbor – but that didn't matter much when there were only a few dates to ship out and tins to ship in. Soon the entire modern world was dumped into the sand – air conditioners and deep freezers, timber and steel, concrete and pipe and typewriters and filing cabinets. Anything one could imagine could be found there, sweeping in on the Arabian shore. Everything would have to be carried ashore by hand until a port, Mina Zayed, and airport were completed in 1969. Everything was half-formed and half the time the cargo ships had to line up for miles to deposit their freight, sometimes waiting for months at a time.

With every jetliner that landed in Abu Dhabi came the vultures of world commerce, bankers and businessmen, all offering their services and all trying to get their hands on a piece of Zayed's annual income of $100 million dollars. The machines that came ashore on the beach pounded the desert into new shapes and the men who descended from the airplanes helped in drafting a new world. They knew nothing about the old Arabia. To them, it was just another job.

As the old *barasti* huts were pulled down, Zayed gave every Abu Dhabian three or four pieces of land, for a home, commercial building, industrial project and a farm. To the budding farmers, he gave irrigation equipment and tractors. Soon there were four and five-floor office blocks instead of shanties and concrete instead of mud. Not so long before there wasn't a single bank in Abu Dhabi; soon there were rows of them.

The modern world began to take over.

Soon the government would be subsidizing almost every aspect of life. Schools where boys memorized the Qur'an had been the only education most children had ever known. There had not been a hospital in Abu Dhabi until a few years earlier, when it was still a place full of desperate poverty and sickness. Many, from the youngest child to the oldest man, suffered eye ailments, usually trachoma, of one type or another. Many suffered from tuberculosis. Every jab with a syringe became a sort of revelation. Zayed would build hospitals and schools and universities and set aside overseas scholarships for the brightest.

To reward his cousin Sheikh Mohammed bin Khalifa for his support, since the latter was still the leader of the Bani Khalifa branch of the ruling family, Zayed made him head of the "family council." Zayed also gave key positions of state to Sheikh Mohammed's sons as follows: Hamdan, Governor of Das Island since 1957, became in charge of all public works, and in 1967, Hamdan also became in charge of the entire civil administration, which effectively made him a first deputy prime minister. Mubarak became in charge of security, a post he already had under Shakhbut but which was not defined formally. Tahnoon became Zayed's representative in Al-Ain as well as in charge of the oil sector. Saif became in charge of planning. Surour became Zayed's chamberlain, a close adviser and eventually was given Zayed's favorite daughter in marriage.

Unlike the miserly Shakhbut, Zayed provided his Bani Khalifa cousins with more traditional compensation, liberal stipends. By 1970 the sheikhs of the Al-Nahyan received, by one estimate, at least 25 percent of the total oil revenues.

Zayed tried to strike a balance between building the new and wrecking the old. He knew from experience that if he was too slow to tear down the old world he might be removed like Shakhbut. But if he tried to construct the new world too quickly he may destroy himself just as surely. Life for Zayed had become a perpetual balancing act, between the personal leadership of the past and the faceless, impersonal administration of the future. Like Shakhbut he still held a majlis every day so that his people could meet him, talk to him and complain to him in the traditional desert way.

The ritual remained unchanged. The coffee was served; time, motion and people seemed as leisurely as ever. But behind the appearance of tradition, the modern world was creeping in. When Zayed was simply the leader of a tribe men could meet him every day; now he was the administrator of a modern state. The majlis did not last all morning anymore. Zayed could only offer his people an hour or so of his time, and even that was interrupted by the demands of the modern world. He was forced to shut them out of his life. They could only wait while the world moved in.

Now Zayed had to play host to international businessman and financiers, planners, to scientists and technocrats, the courtesies of the old world mingling with the business of the new. Zayed would host a fair number of con men, too, unable to pick them from the rest. Soon it was not the tribal retainers but the newcomers in business suits that got the place of honor at Zayed's side. They were there because they represented the power to provide the people of Abu Dhabi with anything Zayed could now afford to buy.

Zayed heard their proposals for projects – some good, some dubious but always expensive. Yet the old ritual went on, balancing the new with the old. The first thing the western newcomers had to learn was patience. Arabs could sit for hours in the majlis and never do anything but inquire after each other's health. All in good time and all by the will of God. Never do today what you can defer until tomorrow. When a tribesman with a dilemma came to Zayed to sort it out everyone else had to wait.

Patience and still more patience. But money waited for no one and burned holes in patience. It might have been the will of God that gave Abu Dhabi its wealth, but it was the will of Zayed that has to decide what to do now. In the new Arabia time was money. It was a world where time and opportunity had changed places. Yesterday time seemed endless and opportunity stymied; today time short and opportunity bountiful. Zayed was known to say that he didn't know what would happen in ten years' time but he felt that he must give everything to his people now because they had had nothing for so long.

Zayed knew that his money would change everything. The first thing to go would be the Arabs' love for his camel, but what is a camel compared to a jet aircraft. Zayed's life was now ruled by a few imperatives: decide, choose and act. The pressure sometimes caused him to act harshly and hastily. When the planners showed him a small scale model for a new souk he dismissed months of work with barely a moment's thought. "No. Take it away and start again," he said with a wave of his hand. In his office, Zayed was the modern oil tycoon, aloof and decisive, but as he walked into the courtyard of the palace the centuries slid back. Now he was back to the role of sheikh, the paterfamilias to his people, the feudal lord trailed by his followers in procession to the daily feast. In the courtyard time still seemed endless and patience more so.

To the tribesmen of the desert used to dates and bread baked in the sand, Zayed's table was a revelation. Money left its mark there too. The table was loaded with more food than many of them had ever seen and it was a table rather than the floor. The idea of a free meal for Zayed's followers was traditional and he rarely sat down with less than fifty men. But the forms and the food were new. Waiters in black ties, the plates and soup spoons, a completely new ritual of table manners to master. Like the nouveau riche everywhere Abu Dhabians struggled to keep up.

1968 WAS A WHIRLWIND by the old standards. Zayed embarked upon a £350 million ($840 million) five-year development plan. Abu Dhabi city was a vast building site, crisscrossed by trenches, chugging bulldozers raising clouds of dust, foundations, and bare steel ribs on every side. It seemed that everything was being built at once. In fact, it was. Money was no object. The first sewers were going in along with the first hotel swimming pool. Neon lit highways were being laid where only dusty tracks had existed before. In January aircraft landed on a flattened stretch of sand. Terminal buildings rose from the sand and by July planes took off from an international airport built to accommodate the Concorde. With the care and occasional caprice of a boy in a toy store, Zayed was buying the infrastructure of a modern community for his astonished people.

The days when a ruler had so little money that nobody cared how he spent it were over. Now Zayed needed to have a budget and a British accountant to keep the books. Every dollar spent was another nail in the coffin of the Arabia Thesiger had visited and maybe in the life of Zayed too. Soon enough Zayed was a little less sure of himself. He could ask new questions and make new demands, but who could give him the answers? Not even Zayed's best friends could tell him how the story would end, happily or as a parody.

With their uncertainty about the new way of life, Zayed and his men, with increasing frequency, went back to the desert as often as they could. The desert was still home – the place he knew before he was rich and the only place he would really know until the day he died. In the desert, for a day, or a week, or a month, Zayed and his men could revert to the old and simpler ways, to a genuine sense of comradeship that the modern world left no time for. It was a place without budgets or civil servants, without figures, complications or closed office doors. There was only the sky, the heat, the emptiness, and the infinity of time that they had always understood. Out there they can all be sure of themselves; they can relax and be men again.

Even Zayed could relax there and be one of the boys, and fight a mock battle with one of his aides.

A trip to the desert was a recovery of innocence, a return to Eden. But like all escapes, it was also an illusion. The innocence was lost and would never be recaptured because the old Arabia of mystery and isolation, hardship and tribal war had been swept into the modern world at last.

Some Arabs, like Shakhbut, would continue to fight a rearguard action against the assaults of the modern world but it was too late. There was not even a choice between the old life and the new. God and the oil companies had already chosen for them. There was no going back. The relentless tide of the century in which they lived did not tolerate it.

One of the last of the isolated lands was giving up its old anonymity and had been uncovered and dragged naked into the world's sight. From then on the people of Arabia, like all of us, would have to face the infinite hopes, possibilities, and disillusionments of the modern world.

UNITIES

ROME WAS NOT built in a day. Neither was Abu Dhabi, although it felt that way at times. With his new city unfolding before him, Zayed had already set himself to a much more difficult task – convincing the rulers of the neighboring sheikhdoms to join Abu Dhabi in forming a modern nation.

In those early years of flux, some changes took hold more quickly than others. Zayed still liked to drive himself, piloting a struggling black Chrysler up and over the undulating dunes. Zayed did not like to be physically alone. The undisputed boss to the tribesmen who seemingly followed him everywhere, he was the man to serve, to hunt with and to fight for. His forebears ruled the desert from the back of a camel. Now he rode it in a limousine. But he remained, like all of his ancestors, the center of tribal life. Those who did not travel with Zayed came out of the desert on camels to greet him. They all owed their loyalty to him and all expected rewards from him.

Though he was now a multi-millionaire, one of Arabia's nouveau riche, Zayed's tastes were not influenced much by his money. He liked the simple life, everything which was slipping away: to drive himself, to go hunting and camping in the desert, to be with his people and to follow the ways of the Arabia of his youth. And yet it was unavoidable that money, something none of them had ever known before, began to leave its mark everywhere, from the ruler – who got millions – to the soldier or laborer who got mere scraps, but it bought a new life for both of them.

Twenty years before Zayed would have hunted game on foot, with only a few falcons to help him. Now he took up to a hundred birds on his hunting trips. Each of Zayed's followers had a falcon to care for: they trained them, stroked them and talked to them. Like racehorses, they are the pampered pets of a rich man's camp. And like racehorses, they cost big money. A good bird cost $600 or more, imported from Syria or Iraq. And with so much oil money in Arabia, the price was rising every year.

Nothing escaped the touch of money.

One of Zayed's first acts was to give away all the money that Shakhbut had hoarded. He announced that anyone in the seven emirates who needed cash should come to see him. And they came to Abu Dhabi on foot, by camel, car, or dhow and Zayed made his handouts until the coffers were emptied. Some thought it a crazy gesture but it was Zayed's generosity that paved the way toward wielding those disparate sheikhdoms into a nation. He became the paternal kindly sheikh, personally available to his people, and no one could compete, certainly not the has-beens in Sharjah or the commercial upstarts in Dubai. Later they asked for overseas medical treatment, a house, or pardon for a jailed relative. The handlers at the royal court compiled lists of names and went door to door with handouts of cash. In such ways, Zayed built a nation. Some thought that he was wasting money but they couldn't argue once it started to buy loyalty for the union.

In the months after his accession Zayed set out on a tour of the other emirates, a ritual he would continue every year of his reign. In the footage of his visit to a neighbor, the ruler of the dust bowl town of Fujairah, there was little evocation of modernity. Zayed sat with tribesmen smoking *dokha*, flavored Iranian tobacco with the consistency of dried herbs, from a *midwakh*, a traditional pipe made out of wood or bone. Superficially the old customs were unchanged. The tent went up as it always had and the food was prepared in large black kettles as simply as before. As the meat stewed in the kettles, Zayed took several small cups of coffee from a follower.

His natural pace remained leisurely, almost intimate. Time was about the only thing the desert has been rich in before oil. Time for coffee and talk, time made into ritual from century to century, from morning until night.

Before long the feast was ready and Zayed took his place on the carpet next to his host, one the poorest rulers on the coast. The feast was traditional – goat's meat, chicken and rice, placed before them on a white tray as long as a man. Hands ripped meat and bones off carcasses as servants distribute food to each guest. Now that Zayed was a rich man a traditional feast became an offering to a benefactor instead. Unlike many of Arabia's oil millionaires, Zayed believed in sharing his wealth. He believed that the oil business was like a lottery: I might still be poor and my neighbors might be rich so we should help each other. Zayed was fed and his host was no longer quite so poor. Finished, Zayed crouched to the side of the room as a servant poured water from a kettle into a shallow bowl. Zayed washed his hands and brushed his teeth with a finger before wiping his hands on a towel held by a servant.

Finally, when the VIPs were finished their followers moved in, forming strips of meat and rice into balls and popping them into their mouths. There would be several groups of the poor to come, one after another, sharing in the less than elegant spectacle of a blowout feast laid out on a rich man's floor. By the end, bones and scrap and scattered bits of rice would be all that remained in the tray.

Some things remained impervious to change. Nostalgia for a world not long departed continued to pull at the heart, the world where Zayed was raised and where he always preferred to be: around the campfire in the cool desert night among his men, listening to endless Arab fairytales, stories about love and beauty and heroism, stories the audience knew as well as the storyteller. It was how they had passed time for a thousand years.

Girls swung their hair, and the men chanted hour after hour. Sometimes Zayed's eyes narrowed and glazed over as his mind drifted into contemplation and reflection. When the fairy tale was over, the men would clap and take coffee from small, handless white cups. In the desert, there was no rush. At least that is how it used to be, but Zayed had begun to learn better.

IT WAS AT FEASTS and informal gatherings that the real work of union was accomplished. From the early 1960s, Zayed had been of the opinion that a federation of the various emirates was both necessary and inevitable. Shakhbut had never much cared for his fellow rulers or any projects to promote unity. A large part of Zayed's attractiveness to the British was his farsightedness on that very matter. Zayed was of the opinion that

There was no future for the Trucial States at present. They were small and weak and most of them were poor. It was obvious that they would be stronger if they were united in some way and that the whole area would develop and progress if the poorer parts benefited from the richer... [Zayed] would like to see a federation in which the rulers would work for the common good of the area, instead of each for himself as at present.

Unlike elsewhere in Britain's colonies, the British built very little of the standard colonial infrastructure of roads, hospitals, and schools in the lower Gulf sheikhdoms. Though the British had ensured Zayed's assumption of power, they did not treat him very well. In response to anti-colonial sentiments and budgetary pressures, Britain would simply cut and run, leaving the area nearly helpless.

In 1967 British troops were withdrawn from Aden and the Gulf rulers wanted reassurance that the British would maintain their presence. In November, Goronwy Roberts, minister of state at the Foreign Office, visited the Gulf and made the usual promises. By January he was back with an entirely different message: that Britain would withdraw from the Gulf by the end of 1971. The Gulf rulers felt betrayed and vulnerable. Zayed offered to pay the cost of a continuing military presence but the British would not be dissuaded. The rulers would have to make their own arrangements.

In February 1968 Zayed and Rashid agreed on the first steps toward union, establishing a working framework for negotiations that would go on for three years. The proposed union – one country under one flag – would establish inter-emirate cooperation in four matters: foreign affairs, defense and security, services such as health and education, and citizenship and immigration. This accord – the Dubai Agreement – also determined that any of the other seven protected emirates would be welcome to join the federation. Two weeks later, all seven of the other states accepted the agreement.

By publicly taking the initiative the rulers placed themselves in a position of independence from the British. Even Cairo's Voice of the Arabs heralded the announcement as a victory, one which would produce progress in achieving independence from Western imperialism. Within months, the agreement became irrelevant under their mutual suspicions and ambitions.

The agreement quickly disintegrated under the weight of numerous problems not addressed in the relatively vague articles of the initial agreement. The internal dynamics of the various states and their links to the major powers in the region stymied the federation and overshadowed the process for the next three years.

In late May, the nine leaders met in Abu Dhabi to begin clarifying negotiating details: power-sharing among the states, representation, and the location of a future capital. The following day, the meeting ended without any progress and a public announcement postponing future discussions.

From May 1968 until December 1971, the real question was whether or not a federation would come into being at all. The smaller sheikhdoms looked to Zayed out of necessity but the larger ones remained wary. Despite the optimism of those early days, the agreement between Dubai and Abu Dhabi had been tentative from the outset. The effort exerted on Zayed's behalf to bring about Rashid's cooperation created suspicion among the other rulers regarding Zayed's ambitions for his role in the future state.

As part of the agreement with Rashid, Zayed ceded approximately ten miles of Abu Dhabi's seabed to Dubai and also paid Rashid £3 million. This raised concerns among some of the rulers that Zayed was using Abu Dhabi's oil wealth in order to buy influence. The move, seen as an effort to enlarge Zayed's power, aggravated Sheikh Ahmad of Qatar who complained that he saw the move as a "first step" by Zayed in taking over the whole of the Trucial Coast.

Qatar's rulers had been suspicious of Bani Yas expansionism at least since the mid-nineteenth century when the two states had been at war. In 1965 the smaller states had outstripped Qatar's oil production by nearly 20 million barrels. The gap continued to grow exponentially, making it clear that Abu Dhabi's oil wealth and influence in the region would continue to grow. The apparent purchase of an alliance between Abu Dhabi and Dubai confirmed that Qatar's sway was waning. The British also believed Zayed was the main worry and that he had to be persuaded to cooperate and not to dominate.

While Sheikh Ahmad signed the accord and agreed to participate in the initial meeting, his subsequent actions belied his uneasiness. Before the meeting in late May had even taken place, Ahmad seemed to be putting pressure on Rashid to slow any progress toward implementing the Dubai Agreement. The result was that before the May meeting, one British observer noted that relations between Dubai and Abu Dhabi were "as bad as they have ever been."

Relations deteriorated further when Qatar forwarded several proposals to be included in the meeting's agenda. These included the election of a union president; the establishment of a capital; the creation of a union council and its functions; and the discussion and creation of several ministries for the administration of the prospective state.

Qatar's goal seems to have been to force the talks to collapse by placing the remaining states in the position of taking the blame for Qatar leaving. This became more apparent as each state's delegates and advisors prepared for the May 25 meeting. The rulers voted to exclude Qatar's proposals for the agenda of the first meeting. Ahmad nevertheless continued to press for the proposals' inclusion.

Ahmad's bid for leadership or independence from the federation was not the only source of conflict within the sheikhdoms. Suspicions between Zayed and Rashid continued to plague the negotiations well into 1971. The other rulers viewed Zayed's financial gifts with suspicion. In one instance, Abu Dhabi provided funds and police officers to Sheikh Muhammad Al-Sharqi of Fujairah for the purpose of training a Fujairah police force. Both Qatar and Dubai commented that the Abu Dhabi officers in Fujairah wore Abu Dhabi uniforms and that this could amount to an attempt to eliminate Muhammad through the police force and take over Fujairah. Bahrain's Sheikh Issa intimated to the British that he felt alienated and unwelcome in the federation by the other rulers.

The disunity between the nine rulers continued to bog down the federation process through 1971. For a year following the failure of the May 25-26 gathering, the rulers met intermittently in order to regain the momentum they had lost. Subsequent discussions in October and November failed to produce any substantial developments.

ANY MOVES TOWARD federation were complicated by larger regional and international interests. Britain's military and political presence in the Persian Gulf in the twentieth century had established a kind of neutral zone that prevented both Iran and Saudi Arabia from monopolizing the region. Sustaining that buffer between Saudi Arabia and Iran benefited British aims after the military withdrew in 1971.

The British Foreign Office sought to establish a stable federation that would secure the supply of oil from the Gulf and continue to rely on long-standing economic and political ties with the British government. Britain and the nine smaller states required the endorsement and active support of both Iran and Saudi Arabia if any federation were to succeed. Both countries had ambitions to dominate the region, and both countries had territorial, political, and economic ties to the Trucial States.

Saudi Arabia viewed the whole of the Arabian Peninsula as its own sphere of influence and hoped to extend that influence into the Gulf, insisting on a nine-state federation that would include Qatar and Bahrain. Such an arrangement would prevent Abu Dhabi from dominating.

At the same time, Iran was openly defiant towards the federation and its inclusion of Bahrain. The Shah based his objection on Iran's historical claims to Bahrain, which included its location on the median line of the Persian Gulf. Iran also argued that a number of the mid-Gulf Islands were its sovereign territory, bringing it into conflict with Sharjah and Ras Al-Khaimah, the latter of which actually refused to join the UAE until February 1972 in part because of the dispute over those islands.

These two major points of regional conflict stymied the creation of the federation. At that moment, Zayed's biggest problems were with the Saudis, still intent on extending their rule into territory held by Abu Dhabi. When Britain announced the end of its treaty arrangement with the emirates of the lower Gulf in 1968, King Faisal again set his sights on Buraimi, claiming that the area stretching eastward to the coast of Abu Dhabi was rightfully Saudi.

IN APRIL 1967 ZAYED traveled to Riyadh to pay his respects to King Faisal. The visit was a matter of courtesy. Instead of greeting Zayed warmly the Saudis presented him with a new frontier claim, demanding three-quarters of his sheikhdom. The goal was clearly to deprive Abu Dhabi of two oil fields which had been recently discovered along its southern frontier. Zayed told the king he would have to discuss the proposal with his family and took his leave. He never sent a reply.

Surveys in the high dune country south of Liwa had detected the existence of a large oil-bearing structure. This giant oil field straddled both sides of the border. The southern end of the field in Saudi territory was known as Shaybah; the northern extension, in Abu Dhabi, was named Zarrara.

In May 1970 Zayed again went to Riyadh on his own initiative. His goal was to obtain from Faisal his attitude towards the proposed federation of Gulf states. Faisal listened quietly and then abruptly asked what proposals Zayed had brought to end the frontier dispute. Adhering to British advice not to get into territorial issues, Zayed declined to discuss the matter.

Then Faisal produced his own plan. The Saudis would abandon their claims on Buraimi in exchange for western and southern portions of Abu Dhabi. The Saudis wanted Khor al Odeid as an outlet to the lower Gulf, and by claiming the westernmost portion of Zayed's sheikhdom were effectively attempting to cut Abu Dhabi off from Qatar (during negotiations over forming a federation no less). To leave no doubt in Zayed's mind about the seriousness of his intentions, Faisal demanded that the Abu Dhabi Petroleum Company cease drilling in Zarrara – which he claimed to lay in Saudi territory. Otherwise, he would stop them by force. Zayed asked for time and Faisal gave him two weeks to halt drilling and two months to respond to the frontier proposal.

Abu Dhabi had every right to drill in Zarrara and the Saudis had never had the slightest amount of jurisdiction in the area. If Zayed expected unqualified support he would be disappointed. Though the British government had affirmed the Abu Dhabi-Saudi frontier of 1955, and still had an obligation to uphold it, the Foreign Office equivocated. They were determined to withdraw from the Gulf and would not get involved another long, drawn-out attempt to solve a border problem.

Later in May, Zayed informed Faisal that the drilling had ceased on the well-site closest to the border. Faisal shot back insisting that all drilling in the oil field should cease. The Foreign Office advised Zayed not to provoke Faisal's anger. With great reluctance but with little choice, Zayed agreed to stop drilling while allowing the oil company to leave a solitary rig on the Zarrara site as a symbol of defiance.

The British proposed to negotiate on Zayed's behalf, but instead pursued the diplomacy of the souk, bartering away his rights to the highest bidder. At the beginning of 1971 the Foreign Office, having no real influence on the Saudi government, renewed its pressure on Zayed to yield to Faisal's demands. Hypocritical arguments were deployed. Faisal had retreated from his earlier claims (i.e. most of

Zayed's sheikhdom). Now Zayed must reciprocate! He would get a better deal now then after the British had departed. But how could Zayed be sure that concessions wouldn't provoke further Saudi demands or even that the Saudis would respect any agreement once the British were gone?

The Foreign Office was excessively brusque. Zayed had no choice but to trust that Faisal would keep his word and if he did not conclude a settlement by the end of 1971 he would have to face the Saudis on his own afterward. In such circumstances, he would be lucky to be left with a sand dune to call his own.

The Foreign Office made it abundantly clear that if Zayed were to provoke a crisis with the Saudis before the British left the Gulf – now clearly in his interest – absolutely no assistance would be forthcoming. Both Zayed and Faisal would bide their time.

EVEN WITH THE efforts of the Foreign Office envoy, William Luce, and those of Sheikh Zayed and other regional leaders, until the last months of Britain's treaty relationship with the Gulf sheikhdoms, neither the Foreign Office nor the Arabs themselves were certain that a federation of the lower Gulf states would be in place by Britain's withdrawal.

Progress toward federation had begun to take on momentum in 1970 when the British government secured an agreement with the Shah of Iran to hold a United

Nations referendum on the status of Bahrain. It determined the Bahrainis wanted independence.

Iran rescinded its claim to Bahrain and the pathway to Bahrain's membership in the future federation seemed smoothed by the end of 1970. Bahrain's new independent status created an entirely new dilemma. The ruler seemed more hesitant to join the union than before, inclining more toward total independence. Sheikh Issa confessed to Luce that his, "own inclination was for separate independence," but that he was willing to "make compromises" to ensure the union's success.

The idea of independence in Bahrain had taken hold in the minds of both the ruler and the population, while the prospect of sharing sovereignty with Zayed and Ahmed of Qatar became less attractive. In spite of both Issa's and Ahmed's reluctance to make a firm commitment to the nascent federation, Saudi Arabia continued to press for their inclusion. At the end of 1970, they sent another mission to encourage a nine-state agreement but the deadlock remained.

Gulf rulers questioned William Luce in January and February 1971 as to what Britain's actions would be if the federation failed to materialize. Luce responded that the decision to withdraw remained firm whatever the outcome. With Britain's insistence on withdrawal, and Bahrain's determination to be independent becoming increasingly evident, Saudi Arabia eventually capitulated. In August 1971, Bahrain finally declared its independence. Three weeks later, Qatar followed suit.

In many ways, this decision by Bahrain and Qatar tied Faisal's hands. Were he to object openly to the establishment of a subsequent union on the basis of Qatar and Bahrain's independence, he risked being seen as the cause of such a union's failure. This would have been in direct opposition to what he had initially stated as his reasons for supporting a federation of nine: that he did not believe a union would succeed, and that his support for a union of nine would prevent Saudi Arabia for being blamed for what he considered to be the likely failure of the union after its establishment.

The seven remaining Trucial States had, by that time, reconciled themselves to a union and as the British withdrawal date seemed to be closing in, they chose unity over insecure individual independence.

Agreement was reached on a provisional constitution, which specified the name of the new state (the United Arab Emirates), the "temporary" location of its capital in Abu Dhabi, the composition of the flag, and, most importantly, the relationship between the federal entity and the individual emirates and the structure of federal institutions. Articles 116 and 122 guaranteed the federal nature of the state, by leaving all powers to the individual emirates except for those explicitly reserved for the federal government. Thus, sovereignty and most existing political, economic and administrative institutions were left in the hands of the members.

In general, the most effective federal institutions were those that did not exist on the emirate level. The most important of these institutions was the Council of Rulers, representing the supreme authority in the state and consisting of all seven rulers or their deputies. As the highest authority, the council reviews and approves (or disapproves) all important matters within the UAE. Its decisions required a high degree of consensus: approval of at least five of the seven members, including the two most important emirates, Abu Dhabi and Dubai. This gave Zayed and Rashid a veto over policies of the central government. The council was empowered to delegate authority to other institutions. It elects the president and vice-president of the state for five-year terms. The president has the authority to appoint the prime minister, deputy prime ministers and the other members of the cabinet.

In November 1971, on the eve of Britain's departure from the Gulf, Iran seized three small islands – Abu Musa and the greater and lesser Tunbs. Britain declined to intervene as did Zayed, anxious to avoid a confrontation with his powerful neighbor. On December 3, 1971, six of the remaining emirates – Abu Dhabi, Dubai, Sharjah, Ajman, Umm al-Quwain and Fujairah – ended their special treaty relations with Britain and established the United Arab Emirates.

Only Ras Al-Khaimah resisted. But Sheikh Saqr's vocal disagreement about veto power and his resolution to maintain his independence until the Abu Musa and Tunbs dispute was resolved soon faltered. Impotent, little Ras Al-Khaimah had no chance of defending its claims and, nearly two months later, Saqr signed the constitution and joined the United Arab Emirates.

Faisal made no objection to the idea of the federation but continued to refuse to recognize it. This was done to hold a bargaining chip in any future negotiations over the border with Abu Dhabi. He continued to cling to the arcane notion that the rulers of the lower Gulf were mere vassals, squatters in his territory.

The new federation came to life in a world of uncertainties. Zayed's first act as president was to put his military on a state of alert, fearing that the Saudis were planning to attack Abu Dhabi. Troops were deployed in the south near Zarrara and Hawker Hunters patrolled the western border twice a day. The Saudis never came, yet as one observer noted, it certainly seemed that without the British Zayed had grown quite lonely.

Meanwhile, Zayed's new city was appearing. The meager local population had neither the size nor the inclination to provide the necessary skills or labor so Zayed brought in foreign workers to make up the difference. In Abu Dhabi, the tides that opened creeks and shifted shallows were subdued with a breakwater. Millions of tons of rock blasted from the quarries of the Hajar Mountains above Al-Ain created a new barrier for the town. By 1970 the corniche was circled with lights that cast their trail into the nothingness of the desert. The skyline changed almost as quickly as the headlines. Apartment blocks, villas and the first high-rise offices went up in weeks. Half the place was filled with concrete mixers and steel rods lodged into the ground. Deep foundations were laid for four and eight-story blocks so when demand rose the old structures could be demolished and higher ones erected. Leisure clubs and hotels were constructed, opened and staffed in a day. Roads covered the old tracks and wide boulevards had grown out of the once barren sand island.

By 1972 a small but established city had emerged from the sands, with an increasingly diverse population of over 70,000 – almost five times the figure of a decade before. But the desert could not be entirely escaped. Everything was perpetually dusted with sand and the dearth of both rain and groundwater forced a heavy reliance on desalination.

A FEW MONTHS LATER the British took a dim view of the latest venture in Arab unity. They assessed the situation in UAE as "worrying." That it was a miracle that there was any federation at all. They believed there was no doubt that Zayed had been extremely foolish in external policy, alienating Faisal, the Shah of Iran as well as Rashid – essentially currying favor with the wider Arab world which could not help him while neglecting close neighbors who could.

There was a real possibility that Dubai would pull out of the UAE. Regarding the Saudi-Abu Dhabi border, the British believed that the standing Saudi offer was reasonable – a "good deal" for Zayed. But they had less influence to persuade him of that now.

Meanwhile, the Iranians wanted to see Zayed replaced. The British said that course of action was unworkable and noted that Zayed, for all his faults in foreign policy, was extremely popular in Abu Dhabi.

Zayed had that at least, amidst a sea of Saudi predators and pompous Iranians. With few allies and seemingly fewer friends, Zayed forged ahead with his bold, if tenuous, experiment.

SCHISMS

THE UNITED ARAB EMIRATES survived despite all expectations. Yet it was rife with rivalries and tension and internal contradiction. The UAE remained quite fragile as it passed through its infancy. Zayed was the only ruler working to maintain the union and his motives were strictly personal – the aggrandizement of his international image and the dominance of the UAE by Abu Dhabi. Meanwhile, Rashid of Dubai and Saqr of Ras Al-Khaimah were working against the union and on the verge of cooperating with each other to that end. They viewed the federal structure as the personal instrument of Zayed, his means of dominating them.

There was little will among the rulers to face the problem of the federation's security. They were without any guarantees of protection from the strong powers but the rulers somehow believed that they could surmount any crisis that would arise. Zayed was the most anxious of any of them to keep the federation in existence, but he was also the most oppressed by the knowledge of the latent dangers which existed.

For his most pressing problem, Zayed could only resort to appeasement. In August 1974 a compromise was reached over the frontier dispute with Saudi Arabia. In effect, Zayed gave Faisal everything he wanted, giving up a good portion of the western end of his sheikhdom – a 23-

kilometer strip of land near Khor al Odeid and cutting off any land connection between Qatar and the UAE. In the south Zayed conceded the bulk of the Zarrara oil field. The agreement granted Saudi Arabia 80 percent of the land area encompassing the giant oil field, and all the exploration and drilling rights to the structure, including the 20 percent that remained inside UAE territory. In return, the Saudis recognized the UAE and withdrew their baseless claim to Buraimi.

The question remains whether Zayed signed under duress. To this day his sons certainly think so, that the Saudis mistreated Zayed. But the agreement was the price the Saudis insisted on in return for recognizing the new nation. It is entirely possible Zayed feared that if he failed to agree to the 1974 borders, the Emirati federation would be swallowed up by the Saudi state.

In 1975, the UAE made it plain that it had severe reservations about the agreement. Initially, something like 80 percent of the structure was on the UAE side and 20 percent on the Saudi side. Under the 1974 agreement, the proportions were reversed, leaving roughly 20 percent to the UAE and 80 percent to Saudi Arabia.

While Zayed feared both Faisal and the Shah of Iran, he had the money to aspire to be something of a power himself. It was a time ripe with opportunities. Had Zayed gotten too big for his sandals? That is what the other rulers feared. Some who cleaved onto Zayed assumed that Dubai's days as an independent mercantile fiefdom were numbered, that the future was with Zayed. And he wanted a stronger union.

Some advisors thought the loose federation needed to be brought in line with force. Although a sledgehammer approach was recommended, Zayed seemed to judge that he was not in a strong enough position to challenge the northern sheikhs. He could not assume that the possibility of Rashid and the Qawasim sheikhs breaking out of the UAE and forming their own confederation was an empty threat. There was nowhere to turn and Saudi or Iranian assurances were unlikely.

But Zayed did have several assets. The people of the UAE genuinely wanted a union, particularly the citizens of the smaller, poorer sheikhdoms. The merchants also supported the federation, benefiting from the building of roads and the creation of a uniform currency, as did the young, less conditioned by parochial values as the older generation and influenced by the central government's control over the educational system.

Zayed also had a stick, the Abu Dhabi Defense Forces (ADDF) – a preponderant force compared to the toy-soldier outfits of the other sheikhs. The ADDF was responsible to him personally and well-equipped. And Zayed had cut the officer class in on the economic benefits of the oil boom. While it could not deter external threats it could make rogue elements think twice about insurrection. In case of trouble, Zayed would not have hesitated to use it alone. Yet the ADDF's ability to suppress determined resistance in the other sheikhdoms was questionable. While Zayed may have held most of the cards he didn't have quite all of them. Most critically he still needed to play them accurately. An all-out power move against the other sheikhs was risky.

Zayed opted for a more gradualist approach and would press forward toward unification, asking the other sheikhdoms for contributions the federal budget (which they had been unwilling to make). He would push strongly for a new constitution and exclusive federal control of the armed forces.

In spite of those advisers who recommended a crash program, even if it led to a confrontation with the other rulers, to give the federation real strength, Zayed saw time as essentially on his side. He would allow things to proceed organically. In maintaining the new federation, Zayed would sensibly rely on the policies of consensus.

THE NEW FEDERATION was replete with problems. Rapid development had strained the political fabric. The governmental apparatus was feeble. The manpower base was inadequate. The reliance upon foreigners (many of whose loyalty, as well as expertise, was questioned) was heavy. Zayed had not done enough to give the federation a strong and efficient administration, not that that would have been easy in the best of circumstances.

Though the government system was messy and inefficient, it provided a generally benign framework for the UAE's development boom. While development was very uneven among the emirates, Zayed's generous funding of federal projects brought economic activity to even the poorest areas. The most worrisome situation was in Abu Dhabi itself, where enormous revenue outstripped the government's ability to spend or manage it efficiently. Abu Dhabi's oil revenue in 1974 was over $3 billion; in 1975 it was in excess of $4 billion; the following year it was about one billion more.

Some grumbled that Zayed, once considered progressive was now himself slipping behind the times. Yet the weaknesses of Zayed's administration were mostly outweighed in most people's eyes by its merits – generosity, social concern, and liberality. By the middle of the 1970s, the scope for any of the rulers to individually or collectively break out of the federation had steadily eroded. But there were clear weak spots

Rashid, inscrutable as usual, remained convinced Dubai could go it alone and didn't care whether the federation lived or died. Nor did Ras Al-Khaimah. Saqr was intelligent and ambitious, and according to some still heard voices from the past when the Qawasim were classy seafarers who lorded it over the flea-bitten camel herders of Abu Dhabi. Saqr chafed under the monthly stipend Zayed doled out to him, but even he accepted the federation as irreversible and sought greater personal power within the UAE.

At the root of all the problems was a fundamental schism – the basic difference between Zayed and Rashid, their backgrounds and motivations. Zayed, now in his sixties, was a ruler of the traditional bedouin stamp, with all the characteristic guile, charm, pride and impulsive generosity. He was not formally educated and barely literate, but made up for such shortcomings with a certain wisdom and benevolence. His tendency toward verbal platitudes, sometimes delivered in a rather pontifical manner, could lead one to underestimate his native intelligence. Zayed was pious, but a very tolerant man who followed a "live and let live" philosophy.

He was an astute practitioner of tribal family politics and had welcomed and encouraged his country's headlong plunge into modernization. Yet both in terms of temperament and work habits, he was very much of the old tribal school. His style involved a liberal measure of benign neglect. An arbitrary and unsystematic leader, Zayed like to talk to his town planners about the layout of his city spaces but had little patience with the area in between – delegating responsibility systematically, making ministries run properly, building a body of law and regulations to deal with the ongoing economic boom, etc.

With regards to foreign policy, Zayed liked to play the generous sheikh, and the tremendous jump in oil revenue following the 1973 war allowed Zayed to indulge in his personal wont of hobnobbing with Arab statesmen. He very much aspired to the big leagues. They were delighted to receive the fruits of his generosity but the profligate ease with which he dispensed money to foreigners made the other rulers uneasy. Yet his policy helped to give the UAE the stamp of approval in Arab affairs and the good relations he established with Arab radicals probably helped inhibit internal subversion.

Rashid was a quintessential townsman, with soft hands and ready abacus, a merchant who lived by his wits and who had a basic distrust of those who never had to earn their money by their own devices. He was also an expert administrator. Over the years Rashid had wisely delegated ongoing governmental functions to competent people, leaving himself time for efficient consideration of new projects. Yet he kept a microscopic eye on the affairs of his tiny state. There was a saying in Dubai that Rashid knew what every citizen had in his stomach.

He was ruled utmost by practicality. "We have mosques for those who want them," Rashid once said, "and bars for those who want to drink, and jails for those who drink too much." Rashid's greatest fear was that swarms of federal officials and a proliferation of federal laws would endanger Dubai's autonomy and threaten the laissez-faire economics on which it had thrived.

As the paymaster, Zayed was in favor of greater centralization; as a man who survived and thrived on his own, Rashid was a localist and a proponent of what, in American parlance, could be described as "states' rights."

BY 1975 THE old seaside village of thatched palm-frond *barasti* huts was gone and asphalt roads weaved together a well-planned seaside town. One visitor, Edna O'Brien, saw "towers of concrete as far as the eye could see, cranes, tanks, a sense of unfinishedness as if the place had just been dropped higgledy-piggledy from the sky." She mourned the old Arabia that was simply not there anymore and believed the rapid pace of development risked being "oblivious to the past."

By the end of 1975, the UAE had a population of

650,000, three times its size in 1968, and enjoyed most of the comforts the West had to offer. Hospitals, hamburgers, color television, drive-in cinemas and even a take-away Chinese restaurant. The UAE's people had abandoned their fishing creeks and farming villages *en masse* for new lives in the towns. It was most symbolic that Fujairah, the most remote emirate, lying entirely on the east coast beyond the Hajar Mountains, was linked by modern road to the other emirates for the first time that year.

But Zayed was no longer on easy street. The boom was dissipating. He had been frustrated in trying to out-maneuver Rashid in strengthening the federation. Very little had changed in the federal/emirate relationship. In his public appearances, Zayed looked uncharacteristically preoccupied. The manifold cares of running the state were beginning to weigh upon him. Nor did he enjoy the contrast, increasingly visible to everyone, between vigorous and efficient personal administration of rulers in the other emirates and the scene in Abu Dhabi, a jungle of quarreling sheikhs and the jostling for influence on the part of foreign advisors. All of it had made him surly.

Nevertheless, Zayed prepared a major push on the unification of military and security forces, having experts from Jordan, Kuwait and Saudi Arabia write a comprehensive report and submit their recommendations. Rashid and Saqr would procrastinate and dig in against any such merger. They were prepared to concede little ground if any. While logic dictated the merger of all these units, politics prevented it. As modern versions of sheikhly guards, these individual forces not only performed police duties but protected the rulers and their families from attempted coups. Abu Dhabi and Dubai had fought a border war as recently as 1948, and all the sheikhdoms – especially Ras Al-Khaimah and Sharjah – resented Abu Dhabi's newfound wealth and muscle.

Fearing land grabs by his larger neighbors, Zayed began a rapid buildup of his armed forces in the early 1970s. By 1975, the ADDF had grown to 15,000, equipped with 135 armored vehicles, two squadrons of Mirage IIIs and Vs, some Hawker Hunters and helicopters and Rapier and Crotale SAMs. Abu Dhabi also had an Emiri Guard brigade of elite troops, equipped with 18 AMX-30 tanks and some APCs.

Why was Zayed buying so many tanks and Mirages? Rashid saw an over-armed military as providing that much more opportunity for ambitious officers to knock off the sheikhly regime.

Rashid pointed to the "mess" and comedy of errors in the running of Abu Dhabi. The "terrible" corruption. That federal ministries headed by Abu Dhabi sheikhs were models of inefficiency and corruption. That Zayed spent too much time on foreign trips and gave too much money away. That he was not paying attention to what was going on. "He is the last to know anything," said Rashid. Zayed was naive and simple, dominated by and under the sway of cunning expatriate advisors. Nor did Rashid think Abu Dhabi's system for providing electricity and water free of charge made much sense – "the sheikhs get all the water and the poor people get the shortages."

The critical question for Zayed was how sincere the other rulers were in their professions that if only Abu Dhabi cleaned up its own house they would agree to closer integration within the federation. Or was it just a smokescreen to prevent the federation from developing further.

If Zayed attempted to eliminate corruption in Abu Dhabi the axe would fall mainly on his own cousins in the various ministries. Such a course of action could end up undermining the family consensus upon which his own rule depended. And that would only give the other rulers further excuse not to help strengthen the federation. If Zayed forced the issue he could exacerbate isolationist tendencies in the other emirates. Time remained his greatest ally. In any event, there was no optimistic prospect of Zayed moving expeditiously to clean the stables in his own bailiwick. An energetic administrator he was not. And precious few others in Abu Dhabi gave much of a damn.

THE MODERN GOLD RUSH left nothing untouched. Not even the ruler. The rush to modernize led to everything being built in haste. The Ministry of Foreign Affairs began to crumble two years after its completion. Chunks of cement had fallen off the top of the National Bank of Abu Dhabi. Zayed's Manhal Palace had been shoddily constructed and was constantly undergoing repair and maintenance work. Fed up, Zayed had taken to putting up a large tent about 50 yards from the palace. He preferred the cool evening breezes to the air conditioning anyway. There he would lounge comfortably, with his color TV and surrounded by his *khawiya* and hawks.

He had far greater frustrations than a crumbling palace. The federation was integrating too slowly and Zayed blamed Rashid's obstructionism. Speaking with American Ambassador Michael Sterner, Zayed launched into a vigorous attack – Rashid was a "merchant" surrounded by "corrupt" merchants with no vision beyond the profit and loss column at the end of the day. He was content to see traditional values eroded for the sake of commerce. Rashid gave no accounting for his enormous income – in the vicinity of a billion dollars that year. "How long will people put up with that in this day and age?" Zayed asked. Rashid had all the reins of authority in his hands. Yet he was nearly seventy and his sons were "incompetent." Did he think he would live forever?

Zayed wanted integration of the armed forces and for each emirate to give 50 percent of its income to the federal budget. Yet Rashid was blocking everything. Though it was a bitter disappointment, Zayed, bearing the entire burden of the federation, would pull back and wait for a better day. That would take considerably more time than he could ever have envisioned.

Despite Zayed's criticisms, the finances of the Al-Nahyan were only marginally less opaque than those of Dubai and many of his cousins were indeed corrupt, making fortunes during the thrilling boom years. Zayed's tastes remained relatively modest. For his meals, he preferred traditional bedouin fare – bustard, fish, dates and *machbous*, a stew of lamb or chicken served over rice.

The Manhal Palace (which means "Watering-Place") was completed in 1969. It was situated on Airport Road near the Grand Mosque roundabout. Though the grounds were an oasis of trees in a growing desert of concrete, the edifice was often in need of repairs and on one occasion the ceiling collapsed on the dining table. Zayed lived in the Manhal until 1975.

There were three other modern palaces in the city. Zayed's usual residence was Al Bahr (the Sea) Palace on the eastern side of the island overlooking the eastern mangroves. It is still considered to be a restricted area and is right next door to the UAE Navy headquarters. He also spent time at the Al Mushrif Palace and the Al Bateen Palace, also in the capital. When in Al-Ain he lived at his Al Maqam Palace on the Abu Dhabi road and Zakher Palace. Both were on the outskirts of the city. There was also a Presidential Palace at Al-Hili.

IN 1976 ZAYED suffered his biggest setback. The other rulers, avoiding a serious dispute, decided to extend the interim constitution for another five years. Unnecessarily offensive to Zayed in the eyes of some of the other rulers, Rashid flatly refused to discuss a draft of a new constitution during their meetings. The decision inevitably put on ice preparations for a permanent constitution which Zayed's experts had been drafting and struggling over for the previous year. On top of his failure to get a permanent constitution was the petty matter of internal emirate borders. Yet the rulers still fought over tens of meters. That summer Zayed was exasperated and angry. He believed there must be real executive and legislative authority to allow the president to exercise his responsibilities.

In early August 1976, Zayed threatened to step down as UAE president at the expiry of his term in December, unless his authority was reinforced and certain measures were undertaken to enhance the strength of the federal experiment. In November, the Council of Rulers adopted a series of measures along those lines, including steps toward the merger of military and security forces and the formation of a high financial commission to prepare the federal budget and determine each emirate's contribution. The concessions were largely superficial.

As a result, the terms of the president (Zayed) and vice-president (Rashid) were extended for another five years, as was the validity of the provisional constitution. The denouement of the crisis was marked by the formation of a new government at the beginning of 1977. The reduced size of the new cabinet, including less representation from Abu Dhabi, sent a clear message that the emphasis in cabinet selection was to be placed on rationality and competence and less on formulas aimed at representing all emirates. The threat to step down was a largely empty one, a futile gesture. And the changes remained on paper.

With greatly lessened expectations Zayed had more surface success, achieving a formal merger of the separate emirate defense forces. The much-ballyhooed 1976 formal merger created a general staff headquarters, headed by Jordanian general, yet the lines of authority between the various military commands remain blurred. Unification remained only skin-deep, the merger still only on paper: the sheikhdoms continued separate arms-purchasing policies, and effective control over the armed forces located in each emirate remained exclusively in the hands of that emirate's ruler.

Nor was there much progress getting each emirate to give more than a token contribution to the federal budget. A goodly portion of the problems stemmed from the center. Federal ministries had no effective power – when one wanted to get something done in Abu Dhabi one was always directed to Zayed's *diwan*.

The unresolved weaknesses of this loose federation were laid bare for all to see. There was a continuing malaise in the relations of the various emirates throughout the late 1970s. Some of the rulers argued that to make federalism work, the federal government must be separate and distinct from Abu Dhabi. The latter they believed was mismanaged and overloaded with expatriates who had their own special individual or national interest to protect and promote.

Bickering within the Council of Rulers and tension between the pro-federal and anti-federal blocs sparked a similar crisis in 1978-1979. Zayed and the allied rulers of Sharjah, Fujairah, Ajman and Umm al-Quwain pressed for greater progress in federalization, while Rashid of Dubai and Saqr of Ras Al-Khaimah resisted. Zayed's dissatisfaction continued to grow. Rashid and Saqr continued to refuse to surrender "their" defense forces to a general command that would be dominated by Abu

Dhabi. As a result, Zayed took unilateral action. In February 1978, while on his annual hunting trip to the Cholistan desert in Punjab, Zayed issued a presidential decree tightening federal control over defense matters, providing for the unification of all land, sea and air forces of the UAE and for the abolition of regional commands. Zayed's son Sultan was promoted to brigadier general and named as commander-in-chief. The Sandhurst-educated Sultan was in his mid-twenties and was regarded as bright and serious but also ambitious and arrogant.

The appointment of Sultan, widely seen as inexperienced and unqualified, as commander-in-chief of the UAE Armed Forces provoked the rage of Rashid, who questioned the constitutionality of the selection, and Dubai and Ras Al-Khaimah began to pointedly ignore federal government decisions.

BY THE SPRING of 1978 tensions had reached such a pitch that Rashid was threatening to leave the federation. In June he went out of his way to publicly criticize the way in which the UAE was being run. Rashid argued that Zayed was surrounded by unwise if not mischievous advisors and blamed the latter for creating tensions.

"There is no difference between Zayed and myself," Rashid said. "All of the problems are created by hangers-on who raise difficulties in their desire to turn the federation into a corporate state. Zayed has more than once given orders to follow my advice; they then consider it but do not do it." More than once Zayed had offered the

UAE presidency to Rashid who declined, affirming that only Zayed was qualified to hold that post.

But Dubai's prospects were not as rosy as they had once been. Rashid had maintained a haughty aloofness for years, continuing to believe that Dubai could make its own way as an independent principality if necessary. He never bothered to conceal his exasperation at what he saw as the incompetence of the federal government, as well as the uselessness and meddling of its bureaucracy. Nor did he bother to cultivate relations with any larger Arab state. He didn't view Saudi Arabia as a pressing threat and believed that, in the event of the federation's collapse, he could look to Tehran for help to ensure Dubai's independence and prosperity. Then the Shah fell and Rashid was no longer so confident.

In the UAE a new middle class had given rise to new expectations, an awareness of the need for a new political and social superstructure to match the scale of the economic changes. Among the citizens, there was a groundswell of support for a more centralized and more functional federation. The sheikhs were unaware of the depth of the social and economic contradictions that had emerged. Even Zayed was only somewhat aware of the problems.

The Iranian revolution stimulated demands toward further unification of the Emirates and April 1979 saw the first demonstrations in UAE history, demanding total unity, a shift from big economic projects to those that would benefit the citizen, regulations to limit the entry of illegal workers, guarantees for freedom of political thought and the press, and a more equal distribution of wealth. To deal with the deepening rift, the Council of Rulers was forced to meet formally for the first time in three years.

There was a split in the Supreme Council between the unionists and the separatists. Zayed and Sheikh Sultan of Sharjah were in favor of the demands. Rashid and Saqr, shocked by the very idea of demands being made of them, rejected them out of hand. There was great tension for a few weeks and much speculation that Dubai and Ras Al-Khaimah would withdraw. A militant demonstration, directed against Saqr as a separatist, led to incidents between demonstrators and the police.

The impasse was ended only with Saudi and Kuwaiti mediation. As part of the compromise, Rashid took over as prime minister, thus giving Dubai a stronger voice in federal administrative affairs (and forcing Rashid into more direct involvement in UAE matters). Zayed would not have accepted this under normal circumstances. The government resigned and a new one was formed under Rashid, with considerable difficulty, and brushed aside the demands.

The federal budget, in theory, became a more balanced affair with the 1980 agreement of Dubai to join Abu Dhabi in contributing 50 percent of its income to the UAE. A first five-year plan was drawn up, a central bank belatedly created, and a university built. Even though many of the outstanding contentious issues were still to be resolved, they at least seemed to be manageable.

Despite the continuing malaise within the UAE, no one saw the situation as leading to the breakup of the federation. The other rulers wanted a reduced role for the Abu Dhabi bureaucracy but continued to profess attachment to the federal union.

THE FIRST FIFTEEN YEARS of Zayed's reign saw his newfound riches put to work to transform the lives of his people. The unassuming sandbar on which the city sat witnessed one of the most rapid urbanizations in history. The pace of change was unmatched. After countless generations with little change, they went from desert wanderers to city dwellers almost overnight. Roads were paved and buildings rose and water and power coursed through new utility lines. Schools and hospitals were opened to the public. Huts were swept aside in favor of concrete and cinder blocks. Nomads were drawn from the oases of the interior to settle in newly built villas. Abu Dhabi's urbanized population went from zero to almost 99 percent in a mere fifteen years, and they struggled to come to grips with their new identity and urban surroundings.

Some visitors were unimpressed, one of whom described the city as "a kind of Arabian Torremolinos, a bloated, disordered mass of architectural vulgarities and grotesqueries." While Zayed was determined for his people to lack for nothing, he refused to allow continued modernization and progress to obliterate their traditions and culture. In 1977 Zayed placed a moratorium on the construction of private commercial and residential buildings. The next two decades were comparatively calm after the building boom of the previous one. For a time, it seemed that Rashid and Zayed were trying to outbid one another in folly.

Rashid was a highly astute trader, farsighted enough to enlarge his port and build an international airport long before the oil boom. His liberal policy toward banks and foreign merchants assured his city would remain the commercial hub and chief marketplace of the coast. By the late 1970s, however, Rashid was a victim of flattery and the prisoner of his own reputation. When OPEC chose Bahrain's docks to service large oil tankers, Rashid was miffed and he resolved to build the largest port in the Middle East and the largest dry dock in the world. He then laid plans for a grandiose industrial and commercial complex at Jebel Ali, southwest of Dubai city. At its center would be an aluminum smelter which, of course, would be the biggest in the world. There would also be a new international airport.

The expansion was even more marked in Abu Dhabi. The international airport opened less than a decade before had become insufficient and a second was being built. Zayed lavished attention and money on Al-Ain, out of all proportion to the oasis' population. Besides the usual schools, roads, and electricity, he opened Al-Ain University and approved plans for yet another international airport. To eclipse Rashid's grand projects, Zayed chose the village of Ruwais, 150 miles west of the city, for a similar industrial powerhouse. There would be an oil refinery, a petrochemical complex, fertilizer plant and a giant methane-ethane gas plant – all at a staggering cost.

ZAYED HAD ACCEPTED Rashid's growing influence in order to co-opt him into the unionist camp. Putting Rashid in the spotlight put him under pressure to meet the demands of centralization, in order to remain as head of the government. Yet even after he became prime minister, Rashid did not concern himself much with the wider federation.

Frustrated by the last few years and about seventy, Zayed had entered a period of semi-retirement. Age had brought a degree of crustiness. In 1981 he purged the staff at Al-Ain University, remarking that "there was too much liberal thinking going on." By then Abu Dhabi was mired in mistakes of its own doing and Zayed was becoming progressively more isolated from his people by his own courtiers. Gone were the days when his people could drop in to see him without an appointment.

Arab carpetbaggers of every origin and description had swarmed to enjoy the cornucopia, or feed at the trough, invariably ignorant of Abu Dhabi's past, traditions, and even the geography of Arabia itself and arrogant and condescending toward the natives. A coup by these northern Arab émigrés, insulted by the idea of so much wealth in the hands of a backward bedouin, was the chief potential threat to Al-Nahyan rule. The Abu Dhabi Defense Force could easily crush the émigrés if they acted alone. If the ADDF, or a large part of it, became disaffected, whether alone or allied with the northern Arabs, the ruling house would certainly fall. It was doubtful that the local tribes could resist such a coup. The only certainty was that revolutionary change would mean a great deal of bloodshed. Zayed took precautions. In the late 1970s, his personal protection was entrusted to a contingent of a thousand Moroccan soldiers commanded by General Hamidou Laanigri and provided by the Moroccan king.

Meanwhile, Zayed faced a nascent threat from the most unexpected of sources. In 1982 the 27-year old Sultan bin Zayed, his preferred son, was fired from his position as commander in chief of the armed forces. Sultan had a history of alcohol and chemical dependency and would spend some time in psychiatric institutions.

One story holds that there was an incident with a girl and a shooting and Zayed demanded that Sultan be brought to him "dead or alive." But since Sultan was sent into exile for an indefinite period, some believe that some form of serious divide had emerged.

In the early nineteenth century, the aging Sheikh Shakhbut bin Dhiyab was deposed by his sons and continued to offer support and advice to them for almost two decades. Some locals believe that Sultan bin Zayed tried to overthrow or sideline his father, given the many precedents in the family's history. If Sultan had attempted such a move he was perhaps egged on by bad advice. Zayed, the driving forces behind both Abu Dhabi and the emerging federal state, could never have been so moved aside.

VULTURES

JUST AS SHEIKH RASHID began to play a larger role in the federation his punishing work schedule caught up with him. A few days after hosting a banquet for Indian Prime Minister Indira Gandhi he suffered a severe stroke in May 1981. Though many thought his analysis of the situation in the capital was exaggerated Rashid, for all his pridefulness and blinders, had been extremely perceptive. He was not the type of man to hitch his wagon to a bad investment. And any prescient investor in the late 1970s would have had many reasons to short Abu Dhabi.

The atmosphere in Zayed's Abu Dhabi in those years recalled the Wild West. The building boom was prodigious: a gleaming international airport, dozens of new glass and steel high-rise buildings, parks everywhere. Every morning ubiquitous water trucks, manned by poor Baluchis, planted Zayed's trees and watered the city into existence. The sheer speed of development made it a wonderful hunting ground for flim-flam artists and charlatans. Thousands of Egyptian, Palestinian, Syrian and Iraqi self-seekers infested local and federal bureaucracies and conspired among themselves for position, money or advantage. Zayed's instinctive bedouin generosity and aspirations to be a larger player on the world stage made him highly vulnerable to such types.

Of Abu Dhabi in the 1970s, one historian wrote: "Zayed's court is packed with a host of imposters, intriguers, sycophants and flaneurs (most of them northern Arabs), who ceaselessly jostle with one another for his attention and favor. Flattering, wheedling, shamelessly soliciting for personal ends, they swarm about the person of the ruler like so many flies, constantly striving to gain his ear and deny it to others not of their number, shutting him off more and more from his own people, and even from reality itself."

Many Americans staying at some of his new four-star hotels used to joke that Zayed was the "Jed Clampett of the Middle East." There is a great deal of truth to that. Zayed had spent most of his life as a prince of a tiny corner of a small oasis in a destitute country. He was not modern in any sense of the word. He knew nothing about money, banking or business – in short, a financial ingénue. The palaces were built yet he was simply not aware that most of the people who came offering their services were fortune seekers, quite often dishonest ones at that. He never quite managed to be able to tell the con men from the rest.

It was the wealth of Abu Dhabi that lured many such creatures and it had done so from the beginning. Sycophants, fortune seekers, and opportunists had begun to gather outside Zayed's door as soon as he became ruler. Some of these predators bilked him for millions. Zayed and his family were ill-equipped to handle the demands of the modern world. He knew no one inside or outside Abu

Dhabi with the apparent sophistication to handle finances of the magnitude that were being generated by the oil.

He desperately needed assistance. What was he going to do with all that money? One day in 1967, a nattily dressed Pakistani banker introduced himself. The man said he knew the ways of Western money and said that Zayed would find him useful. The sheikh would find him very useful indeed.

AGHA HASAN ABEDI dreamed of building the biggest bank in the world, one focused on the third world. As it stood, he was chairman of United Bank Ltd., a local bank in an underdeveloped country. Pakistan was too small for his ambitions and Abedi dreamt of deposits, the building blocks of empire. He was among the first bankers anywhere to see that dollar deposits from Middle East oil exports would make many people rich.

Abedi's courting of Zayed in those early years was textbook. He was single-minded, persuasive and willing to do anything to please a client. This meant frequent visits and gifts. Zayed liked him from the start. A man from a poor country. A Muslim. A man he could trust. After a few such visits, Zayed took Abedi falconing. This gave the Pakistani an opportunity to cement the relationship for good.

Falconing was Zayed's passion, using trained hawks to hunt the houbara bustard, a sandy-gray bird with a black-and-white crest about the size of a chicken. The houbara's coloration fused so naturally with the desert that they were hard to pick out at fifteen yards, even when one knew they were there. Moreover, they were fast runners, preferring running to flying. The sheikhs considered the little bird an aphrodisiac and some ate one or two a day.

Zayed removed the saker's yellow hood and the bird twitched her head, scanning the horizon. On spotting the bustard, about 200 yards away, she bobbed her head in expectation, three or four times, up-and-down. In less than a minute the bird left his arm and soared toward her prey, flying swiftly and deliberately. A few nesting birds, flapping and screaming, soared from the dunes into the air. All fell quiet and all that could be seen was a white flutter of feathers and tail from behind a mound of sand. The saker made her final swoop, and white feathers flew in the air.

The bustard hunt was not what it once was. By the late 1960s, the houbara had been hunted almost to extinction in the Gulf. Oil money allowed anyone with a Land Rover to play bedu for a day. The sheikhs were near hysteria when the bird disappeared, hurriedly dispatching scouting parties abroad and recruiting French and British scientists to breed the bird in captivity. It soon became a multi-million dollar industry. But the most pressing problem remained unsolved: where could they hunt the bustard now?

Abedi's solution – he always had one – was to invite Zayed to Pakistan, where the vast deserts of Baluchistan and Punjab teemed with houbara. Abedi and his United Bank handled all the details of accommodations, food and entertainment for Zayed's large entourage and through sheer zealousness, the visits were triumphs of logistics.

Zayed found Punjab to his liking. That first visit Zayed slept in a tent. That soon changed. A massive palace with miles-long walls was built in the sandy desert of the Cholistan, about twelve miles south-east of Rahimyar Khan.

And Abedi was there to look after everything. For Zayed, the relationship was worry-free. His relationship with the banker was unique and exceedingly intimate. Abedi had helped him before the windfall when the British and Americans ignored him and seemed to anticipate his every need. Soon Zayed had absolute trust and total confidence in Abedi, and whatever Abedi said or suggested he looked on with favor.

IN THE EARLY 1970s Zayed began to pump deposits into United Bank, then the third-largest bank in Pakistan. Everything was going Abedi's way. Then Bhutto came to power and nationalized the banks. Ever cool and collected, Abedi didn't consider the loss of his bank to be a serious setback. He had another plan.

His relationship with Abu Dhabi and the years he spent courting other ruling families and merchants gave him access. And it was access that a number of big Western banks, hungrily eyeing the Arabian Peninsula, lacked. Abedi, meanwhile, needed credibility in the West. Determined to retain complete control of day-to-day affairs, Abedi wanted a passive partner and found one in Bank of America. In 1972 the deal was struck. Abedi promised BofA entry to Arab oil wealth in exchange for a

30 percent share in the new bank. Then Abedi convinced Zayed to put up another $1.875 million. Abedi could not contain his elation. The new bank, formally incorporated in Luxembourg two years later, was called the Bank of Credit and Commerce International – BCCI.

It is clear that without the House of Nahyan, Abedi's BCCI never could have come into existence. The emirate was the bank's largest depositor and largest borrower, and for most of BCCI's existence, its largest shareholder. For the first decade of BCCI's existence, as much as 50% of the bank's overall assets were from Abu Dhabi and the Al-Nahyan family, whose oil income of about $750 million in the early 1970s skyrocketed to nearly $10 billion a year by the end of the decade.

BCCI handled a substantial portion of Abu Dhabi's oil revenues. Yet oddly enough, at no time while Abedi was in charge did Abu Dhabi hold more than a small share of BCCI's recorded shares. Abu Dhabi appears not to have invested substantial funds in BCCI, but instead to have insisted on guaranteed rates of return for the use of its money. Thus, rather than being a major investor in BCCI, in the early years, Abu Dhabi only agreed to place extremely large sums of money as deposits at the bank, which BCCI used in lieu of capital.

What had begun with bustard hunting trips to Pakistan resulted in Abedi running Zayed's financial life. He was simultaneously manager of billions of Zayed's personal wealth and the chairman of a new bank that was guaranteed assets of hundreds of millions from the beginning. Abedi now had essentially unlimited resources to create BCCI, relying on Zayed's huge deposits to finance his rapid expansion. The result was that BCCI's finances quickly became so intermingled with the finances of Abu Dhabi that it was difficult even for the bank's insiders to determine where one left off and the other began. Whether Abu Dhabi insiders, including Abu Dhabi's representative on BCCI's board of directors, Ghanim Al-Mazroui, knew of this intermingling remains an open question.

Recognizing his dependency, Abedi made sure BCCI catered to whatever Zayed and particularly his family wanted, whenever they wanted it. Several dozen employees were permanently assigned to look after Zayed's palaces and personal interests in Pakistan, Morocco and elsewhere.

Now the bustard hunting trips cost millions. Zayed spent little on himself

AS THE GROWTH of financial institutions exploded in the 1970s so did BCCI. Other banks could not approach its rate of expansion. Within six years of its establishment, BCCI was a $3 billion bank, something on the order of 1200-fold growth. And Abedi – no longer confined to a small storefront in Abu Dhabi – was riding the whirlwind with luxurious offices in London, the mecca of international banking.

As BCCI swept into the 1980s it was for all intents and purposes the most successful bank in the world, with more than $1 billion in new assets every year. Its customers made up an effective who's who of the Persian Gulf.

Western bankers remained skeptical and a nervous Bank of America sold its equity.

This rapid growth unsettled some regulators at the Bank of England. As early as 1982 one internal memo described BCCI as "on its way to becoming the financial equivalent of the SS Titanic!" However, the governor and his bank supervisory team persuaded themselves - for the moment - that ultimate regulatory responsibility for the group lay with Luxembourg, where the bank was incorporated.

If the British were feckless in acting swiftly they were also right to smell a rat. By 1990 BCCI had built a $20 billion empire. But it was a mirage flickering atop quicksand. To detail the astonishing levels of malfeasance at BCCI is well outside of the scope of this work. Suffice it to say that the acronym has since become synonymous with fraud on the most massive and global of scales. It amassed for itself all the wrong titles – the largest corporate criminal enterprise, the largest Ponzi scheme, and the largest bank fraud scandal. A hugely profitable web of illicit activity. It counted dictators, drug traffickers and terrorists among its customers. Most disturbingly, many governments, including the United States, held accounts. Influential members of Washington's political class had ties to BCCI.

The extent of BCCI's crimes, chronicled in detailed American and British investigations – including a landmark report by then Senator John Kerry in 1992 – is astonishing. Financial fraud gone wild, from unrecorded deposits and phony payments to illegal share-buying. The bank specialized in improper loans, disguised by layers of shell companies. So elaborate and expansive was BCCI's deception that it somehow managed to come to secretly control three major American banks. This would all come out later.

If anything, Zayed's reliance on Abedi only deepened during the 1980s. Early in the decade oil prices collapsed and Zayed sought his old friend's advice. This led to the de facto merger of the sheikh's Private Department and BCCI. By the mid-1980s several hundred million had gone missing from the Karachi office. Naturally, that pilfering was quietly hushed up. In 1988 BCCI was indicted for drug money laundering and began to post multimillion-dollar losses. Despite mounting evidence of BCCI's financial mismanagement and criminal activity, the people around Zayed kept him unaware of the bank's true nature. By then Zayed's court was packed with "young turks" from BCCI.

On a state visit to Pakistan in February that year, Zayed was feted by General Zia in high style. At the presidential residence in Lahore, they feasted on mutton kebab, tikkas, fish and biryani. An aide soon appeared and whispered in Zayed's ear that Abedi, who still had broad authority over the investments and finances of the ruling family, had suffered a heart attack and was in critical condition. The dinner ended abruptly as Zayed and the Pakistani president rushed to Abedi's bedside. Zayed put his own plane, equipped with life-support systems and medical equipment, on standby. Abedi was flown to London the next day.

IN JULY 1991 ZAYED was preparing to celebrate the twenty-fifth anniversary of his accession. It was not to be a happy occasion. In early 1990 the accounting firm Price Waterhouse had uncovered major "irregularities" in a damning report on BCCI. But the UAE ruler had no idea how bad things were. Zayed's advisors had kept the truth about BCCI's desperate financial straits and pending criminal charges from the old man.

Now he found himself embroiled in the largest banking fraud in history. On July 5, amidst evidence of widespread fraud, the Bank of England pulled the trigger. BCCI was shut down and its $20 billion in assets were frozen. Of all the depositors turned victims, Zayed was the most viscerally angry. He had been behind the bank since its inception, in person and in finance, but had been betrayed.

Surrounded by people who had benefited from BCCI's activities, Zayed had been coddled into re-capitalizing the flailing bank. Since mid-1990 he had pumped $3 billion in new capital and deposits. That money was gone and would never be recovered. That was not even the worst part. That was the financial rape of Zayed and the Abu Dhabi Investment Authority by BCCI and its allies in the ruler's Private Department. BCCI had favored higher-ups there with largesse, and one of the recipients was whispered to be the director-general and Zayed's number one man – Ghanim Al-Mazroui.

For Zayed, it was the largest single disaster of his life and a stark realization. It was not so much the financial loss that rankled, as the loss of trust and the loss of face. That he had not only entrusted BCCI with his money, but with his honor. That he had been the principal mark in Abedi's con game. All told, Zayed and Abu Dhabi lost an estimated $9 billion in the shutdown of BCCI.

In the UAE the story was kept quiet, with the authorities cutting BCCI-related stories out of newspapers and magazines. Agha Hasan Abedi faced criminal charges in several countries for crimes related to BCCI. He was convicted in absentia in the United Arab Emirates. Yet Pakistani authorities refused to extradite him. He died of heart failure in 1995. The aftermath of the fiasco dragged on for years. Ultimately, a settlement with Abu Dhabi provided almost half of the funds recovered for creditors. Amazingly, the liquidation of the eight UAE branches of BCCI was completed only in June 2013.

Every November to this day Arab sheikhs and princes descend upon Pakistan in fleets of private planes. They come armed with customized weapons, with computers and radar, communication equipment, generators and air conditioners, hundreds of servants and other staff and priceless falcons used to hunt the bird. Some constructed huge desert palaces, surrounded by fortress-like walls. Others lived in elaborate tent cities guarded by legions of troops.

Each winter their hunting fiefdoms in the vast deserts of Baluchistan, Punjab and Sindh became, in effect, Arab principalities. Falconry was once the sport of kings. In the old days, they would hunt the houbara on foot or camelback, trying to outsmart it by using the camel as a shield.

But now the customized vehicles had replaced the camels and palaces replaced tents. The hunters used radar and infrared spotlights to find the bird at night. What was the challenge, or indeed, the thrill? The houbara didn't stand a chance anymore. For a quarter century, the hunting has been intensive and sustained. The hunt had become mass slaughter and the population of houbara is terribly diminished.

As one exasperated Pakistani official said: "None of this would have happened if it hadn't been for Abedi." The few birds that manage to return to their nesting grounds each year are clever or lucky enough to stay in Iran or cross into India, far luckier than those potentates whom a higher power had seen fit to endow with unimaginable wealth they were ill-prepared to manage.

RASHID EVENTUALLY made a partial recovery from his stroke but he was much diminished and his hair had gone white. He spent the second half of the decade in the final stages of terminal illness. Incapable of carrying out his duties, the running of Dubai fell to his sons. His son Maktoum bin Rashid functioned as acting ruler, while the third son, Mohammed bin Rashid, became the real power center, controlling Dubai's police and military, oil production, and ports. Dubai experienced a sort of interregnum in those years. Any major decisions with regard to federation remained on hold while Rashid was still alive. The city looked inward, to business and trading as it had always done, rapidly emerging as the Hong Kong of the Middle East. An old dream of an older man made true. As his life ebbed, Rashid kept an eye on the progress he had begun, sitting outside the Zabeel Palace and watching new skyscrapers going up. Rashid died in his sleep at the age of 84 in October 1990 and was much mourned by his people.

Zayed, meanwhile, remained a robust man well into his seventies. He remained, like many bedouins, a natural poet. His poems, composed on the spot, were written down by his aides. But age could not be warded off forever. He dyed his hair black and had his information officials distribute somewhat dated, more youthful pictures of himself.

Given the acute labor pains that accompanied its birth and the struggles of its infancy, the first twenty years of the federal experiment were a surprising success. Yet integration remained slow throughout the 1980s. On the surface, at least, the process of federalization had slowed to an imperceptible crawl but no one questioned the underlying legitimacy of the federal state. As one diplomat put it, the art of diplomacy in the UAE during those years was finding the government. Zayed, though president of the country, spent considerable time abroad in those years and appeared to have lost most of his past enthusiasm.

Zayed's true passion was for agriculture. "There shall be palm trees and pomegranates, fountains and pleasant gardens..." – the Prophet's depiction of Paradise was Zayed's dream as well. He talked of palm saplings, water resources and new farms in an age of high rise buildings. Zayed's tree planting schemes soon became legendary. If

Zayed wanted a street, he wanted it lined with trees. Parks had to have fountains and flowering gardens. The sheikh also oversaw the construction of twenty public parks in Abu Dhabi. Zayed spent inestimable sums turning Abu Dhabi, once a barren wasteland, into one of the greenest cities in the world. Some 80 million trees would be planted in the emirate, making it the envy of other Arab rulers in the Persian Gulf.

Zayed was enthusiastic about efforts to develop planned communities in the interior of Abu Dhabi. He monitored development and growth by helicopter. If he, during one of his airborne inspections, spotted a dusty settlement below, it was characteristic for him to put down, look around and give instructions for the construction of a clinic, a school, a mosque and thousands of trees.

For fifty miles or so beyond the city both sides of the highway were lined with date palms, *phoenix dactylifera*, several rows deep – one of the few plants that can tolerate the heat. In the desert hinterland, his vast afforestation projects were said to have reduced the searing temperatures by one or two degrees. In replacing the tree cover, Zayed had also encouraged the reappearance of birds and small animals. Killing wildlife was prohibited.

The federation had weathered the crisis of 1978-79, when as Zayed said: "it had been wandering in the troughs of the dunes." Afterwards, the federal process drifted with Zayed's lack of attention. Since Zayed was basically in semi-retirement and Rashid was incapacitated, the result was a crisis of leadership.

The leadership crisis at the federal level was duplicated in the emirates. It was clear that both Abu Dhabi and Dubai would sooner or later face the prospect of a transition to new rulers for the first time since the UAE was formed. The quality of leadership was particularly crucial, given the dual role these successors would face as rulers of rapidly evolving emirates and key players in the future of the federation. Yet the heirs in both cases generated concern, appearing less capable and less interested in affairs of state than their fathers and even less able to get along with each other.

The resolute refusal of the emirates to transfer additional sovereignty to the federal government handicapped, if not paralyzed, many federal bodies. As a result, an abundant number of institutions were duplicated at the emirate level and these usually exercised the real authority within each emirate, as opposed to the paper authority of the federal institution. Even Abu Dhabi demonstrated such prominent examples of duplication as an Executive Council (essentially an Abu Dhabi cabinet).

Moreover, nearly all of the fundamental accomplishments of the federal process dated from the first few years of independence. The constitution remained the original provisional one of 1971, although subsequently amended. The essential administrative structure was unchanged, even though ministers switched chairs and the number of portfolios increased. The reservation of powers not explicitly granted to the UAE government were jealously guarded by all seven emirates and most even sought to take back functions originally granted to the union.

As oil is the predominant source of national income, the emirates were reluctant to give the federal government control over finances. Theoretically, each member was supposed to contribute 50 percent of its income to the federal budget. On a more practical level, this really applied only to the significant oil exporters: Abu Dhabi, Dubai, and later Sharjah. Even in the case of Abu Dhabi, the emirate with by far the largest oil production and therefore the largest income, the federal government was reduced to begging the emirate government for its pledged payments to the federal budget.

When an emirate did honor its commitment to the budget, its actual contribution was minimal since the emirate's expenditure in supposedly federal areas as roads and schools was deducted from the ledger of what it owed the federal government – an old precedent set by Rashid. For all intents and purposes Abu Dhabi, which exported the vast amount of the oil, continued to foot the bill. As a consequence, the federal government was almost completely dependent on the goodwill of the member states to meet its expenses. Defense remained another area of contention. Coordination between the various regional commands remained nonexistent.

The old rivalries, far from subsiding, continued in the attitudes of the ruling families toward each other. There were few among the Al-Nahyan who would even make the effort to speak to members of the Al-Maktoum of Dubai and vice-versa.

Saqr of Ras Al-Khaimah remained as truculent as ever, fighting any extension of federal authority (invariably perceived as Abu Dhabi intriguing), and ever resentful of the turn of fate that had given upstart bedouin great wealth while he, an aristocratic Qasimi, was still powerless and poor. The troubled economic climate of the late 1980s did nothing to improve Saqr's disposition. The resented but essential Abu Dhabi handouts had virtually ceased and various unfinished development projects gave the town of Ras Al-Khaimah a ghost-town look, with its bleak skyline of half-completed hotels, residential blocks and office buildings. Even Al-Qasimi Sharjah expressed growing doubts about its previously pro-federal policy.

There was still considerable feeling in the northern emirates that Abu Dhabi had been too overbearing, insensitive and secretive with the federal budget, especially in defense. A growing resentment of Abu Dhabi policies and habits even led to grudging cooperation between Dubai and Sharjah, as exemplified by the ending of their territorial dispute, Sharjah's supplying of gas to Dubai, and Dubai's support of Sheikh Sultan Al-Qasimi during the 1987 coup crisis. Furthermore, the Abu Dhabi-dominated federal bureaucracy was seen as largely inefficient and even incompetent. That bloated structure was the object of much derision from "Dubai Inc.," which was run much more smoothly and with far fewer people.

THERE WOULD BE no repeat of the constitutional crisis of the late 1970s. The year 1981 had seen not only

Rashid's stroke but the deaths of the elderly rulers of Ajman and Umm al-Quwain. The passage of time, several of the "founding fathers" leaving the stage, and the spirit of compromise fostered by Zayed led to an acceptance of the federation. Dubai had begun to systematically contribute to the federal budget and by 1986 all seven emirates were doing so. Despite temporary spikes in tension, like the abortive coup in Sharjah in 1987, the general direction throughout the 1980s and into the 1990s was toward gradual and incremental cooperation. The very *idea* of the UAE became more deeply embedded in everyday life.

Yet Zayed's long patience – which by then could even be termed partial indifference – eventually bore fruit with the federal project seeing some significant successes in his later years. 1996 was the UAE's twenty-fifth year and proved to be the technical equivalent of both his and the federation's jubilee. It was less a triumph than a long-awaited sigh.

Military unification was finally achieved in 1996 with the merger of the Dubai Defense Force and Ras Al-Khaimah National Guard into the genuinely federal UAE Armed Forces. Fittingly, the long-running constitutional issue was finally laid to rest. The "provisional" aspect of the 1971 document was removed and the reference to Abu Dhabi as the "temporary" capital also was dropped. With both constitution and capital now permanent, the durability of the UAE had been made clear. The federation's very survival made it unique in the Arab experience.

Zayed himself remained every inch the great Arab patriarch. His reign had been long and peaceful and prosperous. Throughout he had made few concessions to the modern ways of government. His perspective was simple: "We believe that wealth in itself is of no value unless it is dedicated to the prosperity and welfare of the people."

Despite his many faults, Zayed had built a prosperous city-state from sand, a place of boulevards, towers and emerald parks. And unlike the dour Saudis and the creeping puritanism that was infiltrating the emirates, particularly Sharjah, Zayed's city-state was a model of tolerance. Abu Dhabi was a haven for western and eastern expats alike. His tenure saw the integration into the UAE of individuals from scores of different nationalities and faiths. Spirits were allowed in Abu Dhabi and women were allowed to drive – they were not, by contrast, in Saudi Arabia. Education and health services were free. No one pays taxes and all earnings of expatriates can be freely transferred to any country and converted into any currency.

Most of the credit for the creation of the UAE, as well as making it a lasting thing, belonged to Zayed. Always steering a middle course, and utilizing a deft combination of timely handouts and the politics of consensus, Zayed managed to maintain good relations with his fellow rulers. Those qualities and Abu Dhabi's wealth had allowed the UAE to survive as a political and economic entity. Zayed prided himself on having fostered the UAE's tolerance and openness and that the literacy rate was over ninety percent. It was surely enough of an accomplishment for any lifetime.

The authority and respect that Zayed commanded were central to the whole project, and many expatriates and foreign Arabs were convinced that when the old ruler disappeared from the scene, the federation would become even shakier.

The old man's priorities were often far less weighty in those later years. Zayed still spent several months a year hunting in Pakistan. By the early 1990s, there was vocal and growing opposition in that country to the mass slaughter of houbara, opposition that did not subside. He began to consider going to Morocco instead, where the family had palaces at Oum Azza in the hills south of Rabat, and where another species of the bustard wintered.

During the last leg of his life, beginning around 1992, Zayed was ineffective in the Emirates' day-to-day decision making. By then the open-door policy adopted by Zayed between the ruler and the ruled had gone to oblivion. Now an octogenarian, Zayed was beset by a variety of health problems. In 1996 he underwent minor neck surgery at Mayo Clinic to remove excess cartilage in one of his vertebrae. He spent a month recovering in Minnesota. Yet Zayed remained indomitable, largely hale and hearty until the last year or so of his life.

The entire Middle East was stagnated in gerontocracy in those years, many of the old rulers spending increasing amounts of their time in Morocco, Switzerland and the Costa del Sol. There was wide-ranging speculation about the next generation of rulers. In 1995 Sheikh Hamad bin Khalifa Al-Thani of Qatar ousted his increasingly absent and feckless father Sheikh Khalifa from power in Doha.

Both Saudi King Fahd and Zayed regarded the family coup as a dangerous precedent to the ruling families of the Gulf and plotted against the new Qatari ruler. The two countries organized several hundred tribesmen for a mission to murder Hamad and two of his brothers and restore the old emir. The UAE put fighter aircraft and attack helicopters on alert to support the attempt, which failed when one of the tribesmen betrayed the plot hours before it was to take place.

The old patriarchal concern was now enhanced by a degree of imperiousness. Zayed had decreed that no trees should be cut down in the UAE under any circumstances. And everyone knew Zayed kept meticulous track of his beloved trees. This meant that construction companies had to coordinate with his personal security detail to temporarily unearth trees during the night and replant them before the old man woke up.

On one occasion the electricity went out in Abu Dhabi, a very rare occurrence in the country. Zayed's palace had backup generators but the power outage dragged on and he became angrier by the hour. His security drove him to pick up the official in charge of Abu Dhabi's power plant. Zayed said nothing as they drove out to the plant but it was clear he was seething. When they arrived he told the man to take off his shoes. The man did as he was told. "You can walk back, and get a taste of the misery you are causing my subjects."

HAWKS

THE MILLENNIUM CAME and went and twilight began to settle on the old man. Reports in early 1998 that Zayed was suffering from senile dementia intensified the uncertainty over the succession issue in Abu Dhabi. The health watch continued. Zayed had a kidney transplant in 2000, and his gall bladder removed and minor surgery for a hernia in 2003. All of that was in addition to a chronic problem with edema in his legs.

Zayed's public appearances dwindled and when he was seen his eyes were masked by dark aviator glasses, his grizzled countenance hidden by the tinted glass of his motorcade. Back to Al-Ain, to the sights and sounds of his youth, the solace of the desert and the stars at night. The desert. He was happiest there, always would be, falconing, camping with a small group of followers. The product of the primitive and violent life, he had more in common with the Arabia of the medieval period than the strange imperatives of the 20th century. Slaughtered goats and cauldrons of rice cooking on the wood fires. The boys fighting over a raw liver, salted and bloody.

Did he dream of the hunts in the endless wilderness of the Cholistan, the feasts, tearing off meat from roasted bustards to hand to his guests? Or did his mind drift to elegy, to the visceral? Shakhbut, the British, Faisal, Rashid. That thief Abedi? He had outlived all of them, the men who had made up the mosaic of his life. As the inevitability of the transition grew near Zayed's people began to contemplate the future. From sand to skyscrapers in merely a few decades. And probably no one was more astonished than Zayed. A very simple man to the end, his rambling musings took on elegiac tones. Free housing programs, free of cost health care services, even farms had been distributed among the people. All of life's necessities completely free. He had provided them with all of it and invested in them because they couldn't care for themselves, he said. But one day wonders could be made. Or would the coming generations be pampered wastrels? What would come next?

International observers recognized that the future of the UAE was irrevocably tied to the future stability and prosperity of Abu Dhabi, the largest and wealthiest emirate. The succession was now under a spotlight. Zayed had long before named his eldest son, the dull and uncharismatic Sheikh Khalifa bin Zayed, as crown prince and thus as the future president of the federation. Khalifa fully exercised his functions but was diminished by a heart ailment which led to an operation in 1995. He has suffered a speech impediment ever since. Zayed may have anticipated that Khalifa would have trouble following his footsteps and had no shortage of sons to choose from.

Zayed's favorite wife, Fatima bint Mubarak Al-Kitbi, was the most powerful and influential of his wives and the most prominent female figure in the UAE. Fatima was born in the vicinity of Al-Ain and Zayed reportedly first saw his future bride during a traditional dance. They were married in 1960 when Fatima was in her mid-teens. She is illiterate but those who know her say she is intelligent, with a natural dignity and charming modesty. Many locals liked the fact that she was from a small tribe and not educated.

In 1975, while still in her twenties, Fatima founded the UAE General Women's Union, the leading women's organization in the country. For years Fatima advocated for a greater role for women in politics and worked to improve women's education and eliminate illiteracy. She played a key role in promoting the political fortunes of her six sons. They came to control the military, foreign affairs, intelligence, Zayed's private fortune, access and information.

Some Emiratis believed Fatima could have done far more to advance the condition of women and that the GWU merely promoted women's handicrafts. Critics found her arrogant and only concerned for her own. She and her sons acted as the ailing Zayed's gatekeepers, ensuring that no one spoke to him without their approval.

Despite apparent rivalries among the brothers, it was equally clear that none of them would rock the boat when their father was still alive. But what would happen after Zayed's death? The sons of Fatima were clearly the ascending power, derogatorily referred to in some circles as the "secret committee." Sultan bin Zayed, the second son, had been somewhat rehabilitated from the scandals of the 1980s, rising to the position of deputy prime minister. Erratic and bibulous, Sultan had periodic struggles with alcoholism and substance abuse and was widely viewed within the family as unsuited for leadership. Sultan was deeply skeptical of America's intentions in the region, as opposed to the third son, Mohammed bin Zayed – the eldest son of Fatima – with his Western education (Sandhurst) and orientation, who was seen as "America's man."

What if Sultan ever made it into the line of succession? The sons of Fatima were prepared to work against him and told foreign diplomats so. Despite tangible rivalries among the brothers, no one anticipated a violent showdown. "Draw swords? Not them," an expatriate historian told US diplomats. Before long, Sultan was quietly eased aside. The specter of the 1920s Al-Nahyan fratricides still cast a long shadow.

In a move orchestrated by Fatima and her progeny, the capable, charismatic and hard-working Mohammed bin Zayed was made deputy crown prince in November 2003 by Emiri decree. He bore the closest physical resemblance of any of his brothers to their father and inherited much of Zayed's charisma and savvy.

Despite a tendency for over-reaching behavior, Mohammed was respected for his willingness to put Abu Dhabi's interests above his own and, indeed, some speculated that he had been elevated because he was the son least likely to use the emirate's holdings as his personal bank account. Mohammed was also known for his ambition and had been rumored to be resentful of Khalifa's prominence as crown prince. After his elevation, Mohammed went out of his way to ensure his ascendance was not seen as any kind of weakening of Khalifa's position and stressed his personal loyalty both to his revered father and to the crown prince. With his November 2003 decree, Zayed had established a clear line of succession that was positioned to rule well into the 21st century.

By the summer of 2004, Zayed was weakening markedly, and his public appearances became rare. After returning from a private visit to Geneva in July, Zayed did not appear to recognize or acknowledge the sons and grandsons who had come to greet him. This caused widespread dismay in Al-Ain. His sons shielded him from situations where he might be embarrassed by a failure of memory or loss of train of thought. Local contacts confided to US embassy personnel that the nonagenarian Zayed only had a few months to live. His sons had been running the substantive day-to-day operation of Abu Dhabi since the mid-1990s. It was said that he was still "consulted" on major issues likely to come to his attention.

By that fall rumors were flying, among Emiratis and expatriates alike, like a macabre pastime, at cocktail receptions, private dinners, coffee shops, sports events, and in the hallways of foreign embassies. It was speculated that the newspapers were using file photos.

Without any official confirmation one way or the other of Zayed's health status, all of them were left to watch and listen for telltale signs or hints. Whenever people saw official government vehicles speeding up the freeway from Abu Dhabi to Al-Ain, some would jump to the conclusion that the ruling family was gathering around the patriarch's deathbed to bid him farewell.

In the second week of October, there were rumors that Zayed had either passed away during the night or, at best, was receiving life support. The following day, stocks in Union National Bank plunged. Websites relating to pancreatic cancer (Zayed's alleged condition; others said liver cancer) were blocked. Travel reservations were being made, ATMs were emptied, and, in some cases, there was food hoarding.

On the evening of November 2, 2004, a weeping TV reporter made the formal announcement that Zayed had died. Abu Dhabi's muezzins called throughout the night. All businesses were closed immediately. All shops (apart from those supplying basic necessities) closed and switched off their streetlights so as not to be fined. Well into the following day, the muezzins continued their lament, and throughout the afternoon a curfew was placed on motor vehicles being driven in the city.

Given the U.S. presidential election-night broadcast and its lengthy post-result analyses, the news of Zayed's passing was completely buried in the international media. The UAE's various global investors and would-be tourists were conveniently unaware. The state burial took place at the unfinished Grand Mosque, with prayers at the Sheikh Sultan bin Zayed Mosque. Along the route, locals and expats prayed and wept and women threw themselves to the ground as his cortege passed.

Those who visited Abu Dhabi in the months after the funeral could survey the old man's accomplishments. The city sits at the tip of a T-shaped island jutting into the Persian Gulf. Wide tree-lined boulevards run through clusters of utilitarian concrete-slab high-rises and modern mirrored towers. An elegant corniche stretches the length of the city along the coast. There are finely manicured roundabouts, abundant fountains, and more trees than anywhere else on the Gulf. But those visitors found that it was oddly quiet – there was little traffic, few pedestrians, and no nightlife to speak of. That was all about to change.

HOW CAN THERE be anything less for mankind, created as Allah's successors on earth? Our system of government does not derive its authority from man, but is enshrined in our religion and is based on Allah's Book, the Qur'an. What need have we of what others have conjured up? Its teachings are eternal and complete, while the systems conjured up by man are transitory and incomplete."

Zayed's quaint words were filled with both his ideology and foreshadowing. God had put the oil under the ground of his little kingdom and he truly believed it was God's plan for him to allocate it as a wise patron to better the lives of his citizens.

But now it was a new age, with many systems conjured by men with far too much money. His people now believed in money. Abu Dhabi retained the feel of a provincial town and Emiratis had all the superficialities of modernity: luxury cars, air conditioning and expansive villas. What they lacked was substance: a sense of place, cultural institutions and, most of all, validation. Emiratis had been ignored for all of human history and even though they now had means, most of humankind, if they had heard of it at all, regarded Abu Dhabi as a curious name they could not locate on a map.

In the first decade of the 21st-century Dubai raced ahead developing a city-state based entirely on commerce, finance, real estate and luxury tourism. The monomaniacal Sheikh Mohammed bin Rashid Al-Maktoum, who became ruler in 2006, set about transforming Rashid's regional hub into a global one. Mohammed bin Rashid dreamed of the entire world in one city, determined to make Dubai "number one" and on "par with the world's most prestigious financial centers." Mohammed outdid his father through a barely concealed edifice complex. When he built new buildings, he built them higher than any that had gone before and then built more of them. When he built sand islands in the shape of palm trees, full of expensive real estate, he did not build one but three.

At Dubai's peak, the economy was expanding at about 16 percent a year and it had more real estate under development than Shanghai, a city with thirteen times Dubai's population. Bold and urgent economic ambitions were driven partly by old political insecurities, by Dubai's desire to keep its autonomy, and it would soon lead to an overextension of leisure and tourism mega-projects. The city had built an unsustainable, hubristic model.

Abu Dhabi, by comparison, stood still. Zayed's freeze on private construction in 1977 left development to government agencies and the city continued to grow at a moderate pace throughout the next two decades. By the late 1990s development had slowed to a crawl and one businessman remembers weeds growing out of cracked streets. In the city center, crumbling 1970s and 1980s style buildings contrasted with ultra-modern towers. Zayed had grown ill, and no one dared to suggest any sort of radical change. When foreign diplomats, for example, suggested political reforms his sons dissembled: it was too difficult and sensitive an issue to raise with Zayed, given his advanced age and the state of his health. Another problem was that Zayed technically owned all the land and had long insisted that "not a single grain of sand" be sold. Though most citizens received plots of land, transferring ownership required the sheikh's approval. Outsiders could not buy land. That made it difficult to attract foreign investment, especially when oil prices plunged to $18 a barrel in the late 1990s.

With Zayed's death in 2004, the building began again in earnest. The old consciousness of what they lacked remained clear as Emiratis aspired to opulence and influence. They were ready to recast their city for the future, and it would be consciously defined and redefined.

For a half-dozen frantic years, they built with irrational exuberance. In those years there was more construction than in the previous forty combined. Old buildings were swept away with little compunction and less sentimentality. The ruined mud forts and houses, dilapidated old villas, even the apartment blocks of the 1970s. Abu Dhabians found none of it was worth preserving, uncomfortable reminders as they were of simplicity and poverty. The skyline would be constantly dominated by construction cranes and steel pillars. Towering new buildings appeared on an almost monthly basis, patterned with arches, latticework and turquoise glass and with lines following the curves of the Islamic crescent. There would be new skyscrapers, five-star hotels, a souk, museums and hospitals.

One of the first projects to get off the ground was Abu Dhabi's own international carrier, Etihad Airways. The next thing Abu Dhabi needed was a landmark. The answer was the $3 billion Emirates Palace hotel. It was also building what became the third largest mosque in the world.

Located at the entrance of Abu Dhabi, next to the Maqtaa Bridge, the Sheikh Zayed Grand Mosque was constructed entirely of Greek and Italian marble and distinguished by fanciful arches and three giant domes tipped in gold. Zayed's tomb was there. His grave is simple white marble with white stones and an eternal flame alongside. Surrounded by a carved wall, two imams provide oversight with continuous chants, one invoking the other throughout the day and night. Two guards are present at the gate to the tomb.

Then the emirate legalized the sale of land by citizens, and, in some areas, the purchase of 99-year leaseholds by foreigners. Abu Dhabi immediately began to share in the real estate boom Dubai had thrived in since the late 1990s. They diversified into real estate and high-end tourism, as well as development projects around the world. The Abu Dhabi Investment Authority, set up in 1976 to manage the emirate's oil profits, had an estimated $1 trillion invested in world markets.

In 2008 waves from the global credit crunch swamped Dubai and, by early 2009, it was effectively bankrupt. In their post-Zayed vision for diversification, the Al-Nahyan had cast a wider economic net than Dubai and that cautious approach insulated Abu Dhabi from the property bubble dangers that brought Dubai to its knees. During the crisis Abu Dhabi's rulers provided a drip-feed of assistance, putting Dubai through months of pain and humiliation. Abu Dhabi stepped in with a $10 billion bailout later that year. Mohammed bin Rashid's Dubai was exposed for what it was – a strange and tacky coupling of Hong Kong and Vegas, a soulless monument to hyper-excess.

The crisis was, thus far, the pivotal moment of the UAE in the twenty-first century. Yet the unstated price of Abu Dhabi's support would be stiff. The long-term goal was clear – chastening its neighbor and strengthening the federation. Dubai would now have to be more accommodating of Abu Dhabi's wishes. It would have to forgo its independent foreign policy, which had seen it become Iran's outlet to the world. It was the end of Dubai's economic autonomy, which it had fiercely protected. One can imagine old Rashid rolling in his grave.

With staggering levels of growth in its health and education sectors, the UAE began to enjoy the most high-speed development the world has ever known. A new vision, to be implemented by 2030, would diversify away from hydrocarbons and make Abu Dhabi a business, cultural and tourism hub. Nothing was too audacious or too expensive.

THE NEW CROWN PRINCE, Sheikh Mohammed bin Zayed, quickly consolidated power and within a short period, despite deferential noises about his "boss" and elder brother Sheikh Khalifa, became the de facto ruler of the UAE. Widely regarded as a man of action, Mohammed bin Zayed – known locally as MBZ – quickly made his mark in the UAE and abroad. He looked to the future by investing in education, health care and clean energy. Anything to prepare what was now his citizenry for a post-hydrocarbon future.

Today the UAE is a country Zayed himself might not have recognized, and it is constantly reinventing itself. MBZ has maintained the ruling bargain, the patriarch distributing wealth, fostering a dependent elite, and highlighting and, at times, reinventing history for the purposes of legitimacy.

No one could single-handedly fill Zayed's sandals so he was made into an icon. At times a visitor to Abu Dhabi or someone who peruses the local media may question whether Zayed is *actually* dead. And why should he be? The ultimate patriarchal figure, Zayed had been the charismatic and benevolent patriarch and for decades national identity in the UAE had been constructed around him. He took a young country, made up of a fissiparous group of sheikhdoms in an inhospitable land, and using his wealth molded it into a coherent if imperfect union. Given the odds he faced, and all the factors working against the union, it was a defining accomplishment. And the cult of personality outlived him, attaining almost mythical proportions.

Zayed's image is omnipresent and his ubiquitous visage keeps watch from buildings and billboards and from the portraits displayed on the walls of every government office. Roads are renamed after him and other dead relatives. The bookstore shelves are filled with hagiographies. There are posters and musicals about his life. Heritage is a key word. There is no present or future without the past, as Zayed said. Though long dead he became the figurehead for Abu Dhabi's brand. Now his memory exists largely to bless whatever policies the current rulers see fit. He seems to have a relevant view on almost everything. Who, after all, could ever challenge something blessed by the beloved father Zayed?

Zayed could do no wrong, and the new rulers knew this. His sons are ciphers by comparison, and they use his memory to legitimize their own ideas and ambitions. Little is known about them and they live in palaces clustered in a restricted area near the island's southwest corner. The average citizen rarely sees them as they spend considerable time abroad, tend to their business interests, hunt in the deserts of Pakistan and do whatever else billionaires do to pass their time.

Within the family, MBZ had to contend with another inconvenience: well over a dozen squabbling brothers. The sons of Aisha were all slowly removed from positions of influence, and have so far proved to be minor players in the Al-Nahyan political firmament. The sons of Moza proved more resilient. The eldest, Saif, is the powerful

Deputy Prime Minister and Interior Minister. Hamed, the middle son of Moza, is the managing director of the Abu Dhabi Investment Authority, one of the world's largest sovereign wealth funds.

Zayed had been a strict enforcer of family standards and when he died several of his sons' behavior changed for the worse. Nasser was known to enjoy a party lifestyle and died in 2008 when his helicopter crashed into the Gulf. Issa was caught on camera torturing an Afghan trader and then acquitted by an Emirati court after a mockery of a trial.

There is a fierce rivalry going on behind the scenes. Those sheikhs not in central positions of power are usually trying to find ways of becoming more important. It has become an open secret that the senior Al-Nahyan brothers spy on each other to make sure no one is considering a power grab.

Lacking their father's standing or confidence, MBZ and Saif – whose ministry oversees a far-reaching state surveillance system – began to craft a sophisticated police state. The benign liberality of Zayed's time was abandoned. Any chance of far-reaching democratic reforms evaporated. "If we were to have an election in Dubai tomorrow, the Muslim Brotherhood would take over," MBZ told American officials in 2006.

Externally, MBZ looked with disdain at the slovenly Al-Saud in their palaces in Riyadh, geriatric and stultified, as proof that Darwin may have been right about evolution after all. As one leaked American cable stated: *"the UAE privately regards the Kingdom as its second greatest security threat after Iran (Israel is not on the list). This is based on historic enmity between the Wahabi tribes of the Najd and the Maliki Bedouin/merchants of the UAE, as well as deep seated if rarely articulated anxiety about what might happen if Saudi Arabia came under a more fundamentalist regime."*

And MBZ looked suspiciously across the Gulf. No one had any illusions that the UAE's vast wealth could guarantee its immunity. Less than sixty miles away there was expansionist Shi'a Iran, a new Persian Empire with nuclear ambitions, ready to gobble up his glittering confederation. A hardliner and passionately anti-Iran, MBZ carefully courted America as a natural partner against Islamic terrorism, carefully monitoring mosques and schools and cracking down on "fundamentalists" within the UAE. His loyalty to the world's last superpower was rewarded.

With his staunchly hawkish views on Iran, MBZ began a near-obsessive effort to build up his armed forces. As a result, the UAE has become one of the most militarized countries in the world. He authorized massive arms purchases, showering American defense companies with tens of billions and amassing ever-larger amounts of the finest high-tech weaponry. Apaches and Black Hawks, Patriot missiles, "bunker buster" bombs, cruise missiles. The UAE was the first to order the Terminal High Altitude Area Defense (THAAD) anti-missile batteries. Their upgraded force of F-16 fighters are some of the most advanced in the world, and they are now interested in purchasing the F-35 fighter jet. They have also procured advanced early warning systems and built a large underground airbase somewhere in the southern desert of Abu Dhabi, with a hardened shelter to allow the air force to survive a direct assault.

Another of MBZ's projects, set in motion in 2010, was to establish a foreign mercenary battalion, hiring Erik Prince of Blackwater notoriety to recruit and train the force to "conduct special operations missions inside and outside the country, defend oil pipelines and skyscrapers from terrorist attacks, secure nuclear and radioactive materials and put down internal revolt." One of its possible tasks was "urban combat" – i.e. the Emiratis were interested in deploying the battalion to put down potential uprisings inside the country's sprawling labor camps.

With the continuing deterioration of Sheikh Khalifa's health, it was clear that ultimate power rested with the crown prince. MBZ is not the kind of man who takes many chances. As the Colombian and South African recruits were trained behind the concrete and barbed wire of Zayed Military City, the Arab Spring protests broke out. Even in the UAE, despite the outward signs of progress and stability, cracks were emerging, if not in plain sight, and the crown prince would be confronted with one threat he was unprepared to face.

WHIRLWINDS

THIS STORY BEGAN more than three hundred years ago in the backcountry of Abu Dhabi, the original home of the parent clan of the House of Nahyan. They cultivated date palms and roamed the surrounding desert with their herds. Besides hunted game, their staple diet was basically dates and camel's milk. The homes were built from palm trees and goat and camel hair was used to make tents. In those days if a chief couldn't provide for the tribe or guarantee their safety he was "retired" or killed. The desert demanded all its inhabitants adapt.

The sand and sun were as unforgiving then as they are today. The House of Nahyan now finds itself in the 21st century. But how far have they come from the internecine conflicts of the past? The tribe remains more important than the state. At a more fundamental level, the bedrock of society is the family. And one family matters considerably more than any of the others.

Driving out of Abu Dhabi into the salt flats one enters an eerie and savage, blindingly white emptiness, interrupted by the occasional palm-frond home, or *arish*, and camel farm – glimpses of life before oil. After a time, the sea of plains begins to ripple upwards into light orange dunes. Along the way you pass vast numbers of emaciated ghaf and palm trees, struggling against the fierce heat. Zayed planted millions of trees out there, saying that if he planted enough of them the climate would change. But his dream to green the desert was a pipe dream. The authorities stopped watering them and left them to die after Zayed's death.

After a couple of hours driving south, one reaches the Liwa – a 100-kilometer crescent of oases buttressing the northern reaches of the Rub' al Khali dune fields and liberally sprinkled with shady, lush groves. It is made up of nearly three dozen village and hamlet-sized settlements, with a population of just over 20,000. Farms back right up against towering dunes a hundred meters high. Apart from the usually empty five-star hotel, there is a substantial palace in the area. Today it is home to the UAE's most gilded political prisoner.

When his father died, Hamdan bin Zayed – the second son of Fatima – was a rising star within the family. Those who knew him said he had some of the same qualities as his father. Hamdan spent nearly twenty years serving in senior public office after being appointed Minister of State for Foreign Affairs at the age of 27 in 1990. He held that portfolio until 2006, also serving as the country's deputy prime minister between 1997 and 2009.

Highly capable and an engaging interlocutor, Hamdan was viewed by many as the strongest contender to be the next crown prince. Then he was sidelined from power, rumored to have had a drinking problem. After being removed as deputy prime minister in 2009, Hamdan was shipped out to the desert, appointed ruler's representative in the western region. It was a stunning fall from grace. "His father was the father of the nation – he committed to becoming the father of the flea-bitten hole that is Liwa," one source said. Yet Hamdan resolved to develop Liwa and the surrounding towns into a new tourist and investment destination. What came next, confirmed by two anonymous British sources – an investment manager who worked for Hamdan and a former senior banking executive – was one of the most revealing episodes in recent Emirati history.

Hamdan made a pilgrimage to Mecca in 2010 and during the trip became concerned by his own lack of achievement and returned home with a desire to carve a legacy befitting a son of Zayed. He viewed himself as the "conscience" of his brothers, the only one of the sons who desired to keep their father's legacy alive. Soon he became passionate about injustice within the UAE. The concentration of too much wealth at the top. The lack of judicial independence, in spite of the constitution. The poverty in the northern emirates, particularly Ras Al-Khaimah with its dusty streets and poor water supply, bred resentment and support for opposition groups like the Islamist Al-Islah.

All this gave Hamdan reason to believe that there could be support for a power grab based on making the state more inclusive and democratic. Despite his annoyance with the genuine hypocrisy in the Emirates, his motives were as altruistic as they were self-serving. He began to plot a coup to overthrow his brothers.

Along with two unnamed but influential men, Hamdan gave support to a group of a half-dozen young Abu Dhabi sheikhs. They were to develop a plan to turn the country into a constitutional monarchy and turn the advisory

Federal National Council (FNC) into a parliament with full legislative powers. This would fulfill the aim stated in the preamble of the constitution to progress towards "a comprehensive, representative, democratic regime." And Hamdan, as ruler, would oversee such a transition in order to do the right thing by his father. Whether his commitment to bring democracy to the Emirates was more superficial than genuine will never be known.

The plot gathered pace but in July 2011 was uncovered by state surveillance. The plotters had been discussing their plans on their mobiles and on Skype. It remains unclear what happened during this period. But Hamdan became difficult to contact and was prevented from traveling in and out of the country.

In early September Hamdan – angry and "epically frustrated" with "his brothers' constant infighting" – decided to renounce his title and position and flee the country. He soon came under intense pressure from his brothers to reconsider. His plotting was an act of disloyalty but could be sorted out internally. Renouncing his position was more serious. Such an action could not be kept inside the family and would be seen by the public as a message of weakness.

The sons of Zayed moved quickly. Hamdan's assets were frozen and he was indefinitely banned from traveling. He was sent back to the desert and pops up in the news sporadically, meeting the citizens of Liwa or attending the yearly date festival – public appearances as instructed by his brothers. Hamdan remains marooned out there to this day, effectively under house arrest in the Mezaira'a Palace.

His brother Mohammed has been desperate to ensure the story was kept hidden. But it seems to be the missing piece of everything that has happened since.

NO CONDITION is permanent and the world turned. Zayed had managed to keep the weak UAE protected from any potential conquerors until his death, offering the country as an anti-Saddam Hussein, anti-Iran military base for the United States. MBZ continued this policy, offering himself as the staunchest American ally in the region, and then watched in horror through the 2000s as the UAE's strategic usefulness to the United States withered. Saddam was overthrown and then President Obama decided it would be more cost-effective to negotiate with the Iranian ayatollahs than fight them. Protection of the Gulf States no longer seemed worth it and policymakers were obsessed with halting a rising China.

MBZ thought that the Americans took his frail little country for granted. The UAE was surrounded by dangers and needed to have powerful allies that would defend it. Moreover, he was determined to die before the federation. The great fear, of all Sunnis in the Gulf, was the Americans leaving and Obama began that pivot, preparing for negotiations with Iran and presiding over a vast growth in US oil fracking that reduced dependence on the Persian Gulf. American interest in Saudi Arabia and the UAE diminished. For MBZ this set off alarm bells, as did the Arab Spring in 2011 and the Obama Administration's refusal to save old friends like Mubarak of Egypt.

The same summer as his brother Hamdan's abortive plot, Emirati liberals circulated petitions demanding greater representation and democratic reforms. MBZ feared that if they organized protests and gained access to a megaphone in Western media, the US may turn on him as well. Without American protection, he would be exposed to coups or mass protests. The already unruly labor camps might explode and the country's economy might grind to a halt.

MBZ struck hard against Emirati liberals in 2011-12, arresting and torturing them and forcing them to sign pledges that they would never again agitate for democracy. He passed sweeping anti-terrorism laws to imprison or exile opponents. Soon there was an unprecedented crackdown on civil society and any groups calling for reform.

There were other reasons for MBZ's insecurity. Abu Dhabians and even expats looked back with nostalgia on the Zayed era as a simpler, quieter time, a time when Abu Dhabi was more than just money. Zayed remains admired for his piety, his tolerance and relatively liberal rule. Within a decade of Zayed's death that unifying glue had weakened. Zayed was the national symbol of identity and his sons were unable to find a suitable replacement. Instead, they resorted to blaming "the other" – namely Islamists – in order to rally the support of the populace.

MBZ next turned on his old foe, the Muslim Brotherhood, which had seized power in Egypt and then looked like the ascending political force in the Arab world. In a far larger sweep of arrests, MBZ broke up Al-Islah, the UAE branch of the Muslim Brotherhood. Sixty-nine activists were convicted of sedition in what was effectively a show trial. The Emiratis, having never experienced such purges before, were left in a state of shock as MBZ demonstrated his willingness to do whatever necessary to preserve the system his family ruled.

The viciousness of the crackdown against Al-Islah is believed to stem from MBZ's awareness that he was increasingly vulnerable to a palace coup – a plotting prince allied with Islamists. In this scenario, a prince could guarantee tribal support as a constitutional monarch, while the Islamists could provide electoral and popular support in the north. The irony is that such an outcome is fairly in tune with the gradual process expected by the signatories of the constitution, including Zayed himself, who always maintained a good relationship with Al-Islah.

With regards to Iran, MBZ saw that country's nuclear program as the greatest threat to Emirati security and the Iranians as Shi'a imperialists dedicated to spreading their influence to every corner of the region. He first sought to convince Obama to launch an air war. When that failed he tried to nudge the Israelis into striking Iran, knowing the inevitable Iranian retaliation would drag America into the unwanted war he has long wanted. MBZ calculated that a hard American response could cripple the regime in Tehran, perhaps even cause a revolt against it. But the Israelis did not dare make such a move without Washington's consent.

In early 2017, *The Washington Post* reported that MBZ "arranged a secret meeting in January between Blackwater founder Erik Prince and a Russian close to President Vladimir Putin as part of an apparent effort to establish a back-channel line of communication between Moscow and President-elect Donald Trump." The Iranians had grown close to the Russians, especially in supporting Assad in the savage Syrian civil war. For MBZ, facilitating a friendly Russia-America relationship, and getting the Russians to move away from Iran is key.

Things worked out about as well as MBZ could have hoped, as the impulsive amateur in the Oval Office proceeded to rip up the nuclear deal, re-impose sanctions on Tehran and drag America back into a conflict Obama seemingly resolved.

The hostility toward the Shi'a across the Gulf and the Islamist parties at home was matched by a newly aggressive foreign policy. The UAE sent troops to help crush the peaceful Shi'a uprising in Bahrain in 2011; its air force bombed Islamist militias vying to seize the Libyan capital and participated in airstrikes against ISIS in Syria. In Syria, the UAE's muddying of the waters helped to convert a popular uprising into an armed jihadi terrorist campaign.

Following the Arab Spring, it was the UAE that led the renewed plunge into disorder and authoritarianism. The tip of the spear of the counterrevolution. In Egypt MBZ was aggressive in pushing for and financing a reinstatement of military rule, resulting in the 2013 coup that put Abdel Fattah el-Sissi in power in Cairo. Soon the constitution was suspended and peaceful protesters were jailed or massacred. A great deal of Emirati money has flowed to help the new dictator maintain the Egyptian economy. The same kind of thing has been attempted to subvert Tunisia's democracy, as MBZ has allied with the oligarchs to waged a campaign against the moderate, democratic Muslim Brotherhood-affiliated Ennahda party.

Since 2017 Qatar has ridden out a land sea and air blockade by the UAE and Saudi Arabia which was supposed to bring the tiny, progressive state to its knees within days. Yet, apart from a significant financial loss, the Qataris have emerged stronger than before the blockade. But the greatest damage has been done in Yemen, where the UAE's spreading of chaos, in the name of fighting moderate Islamists and militant jihadis, has opened the door to cholera and starvation. The war in Yemen, now in its fourth year, is stalemated with horrible consequences for the Yemeni people.

What began as a proxy conflict – the Saudi-Emirati backed government fighting the Iranian backed Houthis – has through Emirati meddling been fragmented into a multitude of smaller conflicts. Yemen has been reduced to a mishmash of heavily armed fiefdoms and lawless areas, full of warlords, bandits and profiteers.

Across the southern coast the Emiratis have recruited, funded and trained brutal private armies, propped up and allied with secessionist forces, and in effect have created a parallel, client state in South Yemen only answerable to them. The fighting has left Aden further impoverished and chaotic, a broken city of dozens of militias, gutted buildings and refugees.

In short, the UAE has become an exporter of instability in the Middle East and North Africa. And the future will no doubt provide ample opportunity for the House of Nahyan to continue to fish in troubled waters.

THE STATE DEPARTMENT has an official, if rarely used, dissent channel to express contradictory views. All such cables are classified. Policies in Washington are usually motivated by crude domestic politicking not by officers out in the field. Rarely is policy initiated or changed by a knowledgeable expert well-versed in a particular country's political and cultural characteristics. This tendency has been responsible for many misadventures over the last decade and a half. I have no hope of effecting such change. I am not an Arabist in the traditional sense, possessing only rudimentary skills in the language. Yet many years of observation and study have given me a perspective of the region all but unknown in the modern US Foreign Service. What follows is my dissent.

In a Middle East that is coming increasingly unhinged, the UAE has much going for it. The UAE's rulers have been working hard to shape its profile as an emerging regional and global power and, when compared to its neighbors, the federation seems to be the island of calm and prosperity in an ever poorer and more turbulent sea. Yet the UAE's future prosperity is very much an open question.

The last decade has witnessed the upheavals of the Arab Spring, turmoil in Egypt and Tunisia, civil wars in Syria, Libya and Yemen, the crash in oil prices and the Saudis seeming to totter. A pivotal decade with yet unknown implications. The UAE probably has the best prospects of any of the Gulf States. A key factor is the economy. The level of economic development in the Emirates is far higher than in Tunisia, Egypt or Libya. The UAE sits on about 8-10 percent of the world's known oil reserves, almost all of which are in Abu Dhabi. The latter accounts for well over half of the federation's economy. Economic diversification is bearing fruit: in Abu Dhabi, the private sector now accounts for nearly a third of the emirate's GDP. Government-owned vehicles have invested hundreds of billions of dollars abroad.

At the same time, the UAE is more vulnerable than ever to uncontrollable circumstances. Diversification, while superficially successful in reducing dependence on hydrocarbons, has intensified a dependency on foreign economies. In the event of a terrorist attack, invasion or other regional crisis many of the multinationals with branches in the UAE's various free zones would likely close operations and think hard about returning afterward. Similarly, tourist traffic would dwindle if the UAE was no longer seen as being a safe destination.

The federation, given its strategic and commercial significance, had become an increasingly important part of US policy in the Gulf, and despite concerns over human rights abuses, it is widely perceived as one of the most stable countries in the region. The UAE boasts a level of security and stability conspicuously lacking from most of the Middle East. Somehow the country that offers the fewest political freedoms among the Gulf monarchies also enjoys the most stability. Even the Saudis hold token elections. Moreover, unlike the kleptocratic regimes of Mubarak of Egypt or Ben Ali of Tunisia, the UAE is a tribally-based monarchy in which the ruler is obliged to see to the well-being of its people. UAE citizens have it pretty good.

For almost five decades the rulers of the UAE, with Abu Dhabi holding the purse strings, have done a remarkable job of providing for their people, whose standard of living is among the highest in the world. Emiratis remain loyal and the social compact remains in place: the privileged class that makes up only 20 percent of the population, they receive free health care, education and even housing, along with guaranteed monthly salaries and subsidized food and fuel and other services. A large part of the unemployed, levels nowhere near those seen in Egypt or Tunisia, are jobless by choice. Unemployed Emirati youth tend to be driving Lamborghinis instead of running fruit stands. Emiratis naturally tend to avoid conflict and know their rulers are not to be trifled with.

Yet the rulers are hardly without their worries. Even during Zayed's time, political parties were banned and a substantial state security apparatus was erected to guard against unrest. Spend enough time with the politically aware and you will hear grievances ranging from the amount of say they have in how they are governed to rampant nepotism to broken reform promises to the unequal distribution of wealth to fears of being overwhelmed by guest workers. The increasing heavy-handedness of state security has left many, particularly the young, with a feeling of insecurity. The fear of state security prevents people from speaking out about the real injustices in their country.

In certain sections of the population, discontent is simmering, particularly in the northern emirates, which rely upon the federal government (read Abu Dhabi) for energy, housing, hospitals and schools. There are a growing number of unemployed Emiratis, in Ras Al-Khaimah and Sharjah especially, who are becoming second-class citizens in their own country. In the north, there is resentment of the lifestyle and infrastructure of Abu Dhabi and Dubai. While the potential for unrest remains, the prospect of collective action seems remote. How long it stays that way remains an open question. In 2011, with oil prices at $100, Abu Dhabi could afford to spend its way into stability with new handouts and subsidies. Today, with the price of oil hovering in the $60s there is much less room for maneuver.

MOHAMMED BIN ZAYED'S power was only reinforced by Sheikh Khalifa's stroke in early 2014. To a large extent, MBZ and the tight circle around him have already assumed power. He will be Abu Dhabi's next ruler and the UAE's third president. His inner circle includes his full brothers Sheikhs Haza'a, Tahnoon, Abdullah and half-brother Hamed. They are the key players in Abu Dhabi, the ones MBZ trusts to get things done his own particular way, and for better or worse their ambitions and decisions will color and decide the future of their post-modern El

Dorado.

Mohammed bin Zayed is a far tougher, less conciliatory figure than his father, who was renowned for his accommodating style. MBZ and the circle of brothers around him have shown themselves to be insecure and hypersensitive of any form of criticism. They remain the most secretive of dynasties, obsessive about their privacy and uninterested in publicity. The federation has proceeded to suppress any signs of dissent. By sins of commission and omission, they have created fissures in a largely homogenous society that had never before existed.

The Muslim Brotherhood and Al-Islah have been demonized by the rulers and the media and an "us and them" mentality has been created. Yet creating divisions where none had existed is not only dangerous but is a strictly short-term strategy. It does nothing to tackle the root causes of socio-economic discontent. The oppressive approach is actually self-defeating, the disproportionate security response makes the rulers look less credible the eyes of local citizens and international observers alike.

Each new arrest makes it that much harder for the UAE to pose as a tolerant and diverse hub of business and culture, and for a phalanx of the world's foremost cultural and educational institutions to continue to engage with a country that acts so inimically against core freedoms.

But this is not Syria. The UAE *matters* in the coldly realistic perspective and the threshold of western tolerance is higher. And safe to say the West's primary interest is for no country in the world's greatest concentration of readily accessible reserves of hydrocarbons to be controlled by potentially hostile Islamist democracies. Western interests have become implicated in the survival of the Al-Nahyan and the other Gulf regimes.

There is no overt resistance to MBZ within his family, and the only members who could challenge him are his brothers. The only likely candidate would be Sheikh Sultan bin Zayed. I once asked an old Emirati friend about rumors of Sheikh Sultan's opposition to MBZ's elevation. "I wouldn't be surprised. Sheikh Mohammed took the place of Sheikh Sultan who is more loved by his people than Sheikh Mohammed. Sheikh Zayed was a wise man, he knew that one day Sheikh Mohammed would fight for power, so he put him as deputy crown prince, so no fights within the family break out. Sheikh Mohammed always wanted power. Sheikh Zayed's message to him was: your turn will come, just wait."

Though he never fully regained his father's favor after his tumultuous youth, Sheikh Sultan has always paid great personal attention to the tribal elders of the interior, and with Khalifa ailing, maintains a far higher presence in Al-Ain than any his brothers. This is vital given the need to maintain strong ties with the tribes and between the assorted branches of the family. But his outspoken foreign policy views were at odds with his brothers and he vigorously opposed American intervention in Iraq. He paid the price for saying no to America.

Now in his sixties, Sultan bin Zayed is an enigmatic figure and something of a man apart. Sultan refrains from commercial ventures and reportedly is personally repulsed by some of his relatives' corruptibility. He maintains a majlis and private palace at Nahel, in the unspoiled desert about fifty kilometers north of Al-Ain and spends a significant portion of his time there. He regularly consults the tribal elders and each year he sponsors a desert heritage festival with dog and camel races.

Sultan has the most approachable personality of Zayed's sons, and his famously frugal existence and visible disinterest in owning property has earned him the love of the local people. In any event, no one believes that Sultan, out of government for decades, is capable of mounting a challenge against his half-brother Mohammed.

Yet succession in Abu Dhabi is not yet entirely certain. For a time it seemed that Sheikh Haza'a bin Zayed was the next in line to become crown prince. By 2017 two other sheikhs were ascendant within the family. As Chief of UAE State Security from 2016, Sheikh Khaled bin Mohammed bin Zayed, the crown prince's eldest son, has worked to build strong ties with intelligence and military circles in Washington. As his father's chief "securocrat" he has taken an active role in the crackdown on home-grown Islamists, as well as establishing military units in Yemen's southern provinces. In the Governorate of Shabwah he has coordinated with the CIA in fighting Al-Qaeda.

With Sheikh Khaled's rapid ascent there was talk that he had his father's support to succeed him in Abu Dhabi. Soon there was further talk of a concealed conflict between Sheikh Khaled and his uncle UAE National Security Adviser Sheikh Tahnoon bin Zayed, the head of the family-owned conglomerate Royal Group who has cultivated his own extensive security ties and is the preferred choice of the US defense companies. Each sheikh was reported to be actively working to win Washington to his side against the other.

By the end of 2018 differences over succession within the family reached a head. After a series of meetings that December, MBZ allayed his brothers' fears that power would slip from their hands and withdrew his son Sheikh Khaled from contention. All of the sons of Zayed agreed that the transition should be peaceful and that succession would go from brother to brother. They supported Sheikh Tahnoon to be the next crown prince. If Sheikh Tahnoon were to step aside for any reason his brothers plan to meet to choose another from among their ranks. In that case, it would be probable that UAE Foreign Minister Sheikh Abdullah would be selected.

While many are more sanguine about the future of the UAE, I would counsel caution. There are progressive and dynamic thinkers in the royal family but most of them are young or on the periphery of power. There remains a paranoia among the leading sheikhs that if they give too much leeway to dissent, however reasonable, others may start to challenge their authority more and more. The UAE is still a state based on handouts and if those dwindle so will the citizens' loyalty. Emiratis repeat their leaders' mantra of "build while we have the money" but are essentially coddled and lazy, used to a comfortable way of life.

The great danger in the UAE – where Abu Dhabi runs both the government and the security apparatus – is that alienation from the center reinforces and deepens the discontent in the northern emirates. This is a new phase in Emirati politics with very crucial implications for medium-term stability.

In the intermediate to long-term, there are many unknowns. Among Emiratis, it is hard to imagine that protests will be mounted given the various options and opportunities afforded to local citizens. But what if the rulers blatantly overreact to a peaceful protest? What if widespread unrest or insurrection breaks out in the labor camps? What if in Saudi Arabia things start turning sour?

It is impossible to make predictions. Some have recently predicted the imminent collapse of the Gulf monarchies but that seems rash. No one should underestimate their will to power or the repressive lengths they will go to in order to hold that power. The UAE is probably better positioned than most, certainly better than Bahrain or Oman for example, where the next set of rulers will probably have to rely on their armies.

Monarchy, whether constitutional or absolute, has been outdated for two centuries and yet they still exist. They will no doubt continue to exist for some time, especially in the Middle East. Hydrocarbon wealth has allowed them to remain in power long after transformative modernizing forces should have swept them away.

THE HOUSE OF NAHYAN remains one of the world's most powerful families, with wealth to rival Midas. They control the world's largest sovereign wealth fund. Yet the extent of their wealth is difficult to gauge given the fuzzy boundaries between state and royal finances. Their combined holdings are estimated to be worth a trillion dollars or more – far outweighing any of the biggest publicly listed companies and equal to the annual economic output of South Korea or Mexico.

In fifty short years a family of once obscure, nomadic camel-herders rose to become powerful players on the global stage, influencing geopolitics and growing the richest family business now in existence. The rulers of Abu Dhabi are playing a long game, more determined than ever not to be a flash in the pan. To foresee their collapse in the near or even intermediate term is not a bet I would make with confidence.

The Al-Nahyan are thriving and their city is at its apogee. The grand ruling bargain – where they distribute largesse to their inner circle and, to a lesser extent, the general population in return for acquiescence – still holds. But that bargain is threatened by a more empowered citizenry and the looming decline of hydrocarbon reserves. Abu Dhabi has only a few decades of proven oil reserves remaining (over 90 billion barrels) but its rulers are ambitious and have grand plans.

The 2030 masterplan envisions the creation of a knowledge-based economy. This means a heavy focus on education and elite schools such as NYU, MIT and the Sorbonne have set up campuses in the Emirates. All the curricula, of course, is adjusted and watered down to adapt to "local culture."

The UAE continues to do what it is best known for doing – creating land where there was none before. The

Saadiyat Island complex seems to rise out of nowhere, and it is expected to become Abu Dhabi's cultural district. Guggenheim is building its biggest art museum there. Even the Louvre is opening a branch on Saadiyat and will display manuscripts, art, and historical objects spanning millennia. Culture has become a commodity to be purchased.

For some years, Abu Dhabi's rulers have been reducing their reliance on oil and gas by using the spoils to diversify into more sustainable industries. They have invested in infrastructure, green energy, media, transportation, financial services and tourism. Will they be able to sustain the largesse, and thus their legitimacy, under such radically new circumstances? Only time will tell.

For all the talk of its emergence as a "global city," Abu Dhabi is more the modern incarnation of the Renaissance city-state, driven by massive growth in global trade, with the House of Nahyan as an urban political machine, the modern Medici, and their Colombian and South African mercenaries as the new condottiere. Art and business flourished but Tuscany eventually went bankrupt. Family businesses usually fail by the third generation and the Medici ruled for almost 300 years. It was a good run.

But the Al-Nahyan are not the Medici. There is an ephemeral and phony quality to Abu Dhabi and the UAE as a whole. A fake NYU and a fake Sorbonne and a fake MIT. A fake army of imported veteran mercenaries. A fake population – 8 million temporary foreign workers out of 9 million residents. All of it is trending toward fake culture. Money can buy everything in the 21st century it seems, everything except authenticity.

Sooner or later the last barrel of oil will be sold. Mohammed bin Zayed has said he wants to live to see that day and I take him at his word. But long before that happens the efficacy of his strategies will be tested.

The House of Nahyan will not last three hundred years. Over the last decade, the British media has reported extensively how the Al-Nahyan have been buying up chunks of London real estate. This is a wise insurance policy for the future. By the year 2130 it is easy to envision them living in mansions in Knightsbridge and Mayfair reminiscing about their past, the sand having reclaimed their ghost cities, monuments to the wealth and ambitions and follies of a bygone age.

The House of Nahyan – Selected Family Tree

Sheikh Issa bin Nahyan, Chief of the Bani Yas. Father of:

Sheikh Dhiyab bin Issa Al-Nahyan, Ruler of Abu Dhabi c1761-1793, *d.* 1793. Father of:

Sheikh Shakhbut (I) bin Dhiyab Al-Nahyan, Ruler of Abu Dhabi 1793-1816, +1816. Father of:

Sheikh Mohammed bin Shakhbut Al-Nahyan, Ruler of Abu Dhabi 1816-deposed 1818. Brother of:

Sheikh Tahnoon (I) bin Shakhbut Al-Nahyan, Ruler of Abu Dhabi 1818-1833, *d.* 1833. Brother of:

Sheikh Khalifa bin Shakhbut Al-Nahyan, Ruler of Abu Dhabi 1833-1845, *d.* 1845,

Sheikh Issa bin Khaled Al-Nahyan, Ruler of Abu Dhabi 1845, *d.* 1845, from a collateral branch of the family,

Sheikh Dhiyab (II) bin Issa Al-Nahyan, Ruler of Abu Dhabi 1845, *d.* 1845. From a collateral branch of the family,

Sheikh Saeed bin Tahnoon Al-Nahyan, Ruler of Abu Dhabi 1845-deposed 1855. Son of Ruler Tahnoon (I),

Sheikh Zayed (I) bin Khalifa Al-Nahyan, Ruler of Abu Dhabi 1855-1909, *d.* 1909. Son of Ruler Khalifa and father of several sons. Father of:

1909-1912 – Ruler Sheikh Tahnoon (II) bin Zayed Al-Nahyan, Ruler of Abu Dhabi 1909-1912, *d.* 1912. Brother of:

1912-1922 – Ruler Sheikh Hamdan bin Zayed Al-Nahyan, Ruler of Abu Dhabi 1912-1922, *d.* (assassinated) 1922. Brother of:

1922-1926 – Ruler Sheikh Sultan bin Zayed Al-Nahyan, Ruler of Abu Dhabi 1922-1926, *d.* (shot) 1926, *m.* Salaama bint Butti, *d.* 1978. He had issue, four sons and one daughter:
- o 1) H.H. Sheikh Shakhbut (II), Ruler of Abu Dhabi
- o 2) Sheikh Haza'a bin Sultan Al-Nahyan, *b.* 1905, *d.* 1958
- o 3) Sheikh Khaled bin Sultan Al-Nahyan, *b.* 1906, *d.* 1977
- o 4) H.H. Sheikh Zayed (II), Ruler of Abu Dhabi - see below
- o 1) Sheikha Mariam bint Sultan Al-Nahyan

1926-1928 – Ruler Sheikh Saqr bin Zayed Al-Nahyan, Ruler of Abu Dhabi 1926-1928, *d.* (assassinated) 1928. Son of Ruler Zayed (I) and brother of Rulers Tahnoon (II), Hamdan and Sultan. Uncle of:

1928-1966 – Ruler H.H. Sheikh Shakhbut (II) bin Sultan Al-Nahyan, Ruler of Abu Dhabi 1928-6/8/1966. *b.* 1904 *d.* February 1989. Son of Ruler Sheikh Sultan bin Zayed Al-Nahyan. Brother of:

1966 - 2004 – H.H. **Sheikh Zayed** (II) bin Sultan Al-Nahyan, Ruler of Abu Dhabi 6/8/1966-2/11/2004, *b.* Jahili *c.* 1910, son of Ruler Sheikh Sultan bin Zayed Al-Nahyan, Ruler of Abu Dhabi 1922-1926 by his wife, Salaama bint Butti, Abu Dhabi Ruler's Representative in Al-Ain 1946, living in Muwaij'ei, *s.* as Ruler of Abu Dhabi on the abdication of his brother, President of the United Arab Emirates 2/12/1971-2/11/2004, *m.* (first) Sheikha Hussa bint Mohammed bin Khalifa Al-

Nahyan, *m.* (second)... *m.* (third) (*div.*) bint Al-Mashghouni, *m.* (fourth) Moza bint Suhail Al-Khaili, *m.*(fifth) Fatima bint Mubarak Al-Kitbi, *m.*(sixth) Aisha Al-Darmaki, *m.*(seventh) Amna bint Salah Al-Badi, *m.*(eighth). He had issue, 19 sons and 11 daughters:

1) Sheikh Khalifa bin Zayed, Ruler of Abu Dhabi (*s/o* Hussa) – see below
2) Sheikh Sultan bin Zayed, *b.* 1955 (*s/o* bint Al-Mashghouni), *educ.* Cambridge, Royal Military Academy Sandhurst, Lt in the Armed Forces of Abu Dhabi 1973, Asst Chief of Staff 1977, Cdr in Chief of the UAE Armed Forces 1978-1982, Chm of the Public Works Dpt of Abu Dhabi, fmr Deputy Prime Min of the UAE, *m.* 1975 (first) Sheikha Shamsa bint Mohammed bin Khalifa Al-Nahyan. He has issue, 2 sons and 4 daughters:
   - a) Sheikh Haza'a bin Sultan
   - b) Sheikh Khaled bin Sultan
   - a) Sheikha Salaama bint Sultan
   - b) Sheikha Alyazia bint Sultan
   - c) Sheikha Latifa bint Sultan
   - d) Sheikha Mariam bint Sultan
3) Sheikh Mohammed bin Zayed, *b.* 1961 (*s/o* Fatima), *educ.* Royal Military Academy Sandhurst 1979, Commander of the UAE Air Forces and Air Defense 1986, Deputy Chief of Staff of the UAE Armed Forces 1987, Chief of Staff of the UAE Armed Forces 1992-2005, Deputy Crown Prince of Abu Dhabi 2003-2004, Crown Prince of Abu Dhabi November 2004-, Deputy Supreme Commander of the UAE Armed Forces January 2005-, *m.* 1981, Sheikha Salaama bint Hamdan bin Mohammed Al-Nahyan. He has issue, 4 sons and 5 daughters:
   - a) Sheikh Khaled bin Mohammed, Chairman of the State Security Department 2016-, Deputy National Security Advisor 2017-, *m.* 2008 Sheikha Fatima bint Surour bin Mohammed Al-Nahyan
     - a) Sheikh Mohammed, b. 2013, twin
     - a) Sheikha Shamma

- - b) Sheikha Salaama, b. 2013, twin
  - b) Sheikh Dhiyab bin Mohammed, *m.* 2013 Sheikha Latifa bint Hamdan bin Zayed
  - c) Sheikh Hamdan bin Mohammed
  - d) Sheikh Zayed bin Mohammed
  - a) Sheikha Mariam bint Mohammed
  - b) Sheikha Shamsa bint Mohammed
  - c) Sheikha Fatima bint Mohammed
  - d) Sheikha Shamma bint Mohammed
  - e) Sheikha Hussa bint Mohammed

4) Sheikh Hamdan bin Zayed, *b.* 1963 (*s/o* Fatima), *educ.* Al-Ain University (BA Political Science. 1985) Undersecretary at the UAE Foreign Ministry 1985- Minister of State for Foreign Affairs 1990-, Deputy Prime Minister 2003-2009, *m.* 1981 (first) Sheikha Aisha bint Suhail Al-Kitbi. *m.* 1988 (second) Sheikha Shamsa bint Hamdan bin Mohammed Al-Nahyan. He has issue, 6 sons and 3 daughters:

- a) Sheikh Sultan bin Hamdan (*s/o* Aisha)
- b) Sheikh Mohammed bin Hamdan (*s/o* Aisha)
- c) Sheikh Zayed bin Hamdan (*s/o* Shamsa)
- d) Sheikh Yas bin Hamdan (*s/o* Shamsa)
- e) Sheikh Haza'a bin Hamdan (*s/o* Shamsa)
- f) Sheikh Rashid bin Hamdan (*s/o* Shamsa)
- a) Sheikha Fatima bint Hamdan (*s/o* Shamsa)
- b) Sheikha Latifa bint Hamdan (*s/o* Shamsa)
- c) Sheikha Salaama bint Hamdan (*s/o* Shamsa)

5) Sheikh Haza'a bin Zayed, *b.* 1965 (*s/o* Fatima), fmr Chairman of the State Security Department 1992, National Security Advisor 2006, Deputy Chairman of the Abu Dhabi Executive Council 2016, *m.* 1988 Sheikha Moza bint Mohammed bin Butti Al-Hamed. He has issue, 2 sons and 3 daughters:

- a) Sheikh Zayed bin Haza'a
- b) Sheikh Mohammed bin Haza'a
- a) Sheikha Fatima bint Haza'a
- b) Sheikha Salaama bint Haza'a
- c) Sheikha Meera bint Haza'a

6) Sheikh Saeed bin Zayed, *b.* 1965 (*s/o* Aisha), *educ.* UAE University (BA Political Science and Economics.

1988), Undersecretary of Abu Dhabi Planning Department 1988-1991, fmr Chairman of Abu Dhabi Ports Department 1991, *m.* Sheikha Sheikha bint Hamdan bin Mohammed Al-Nahyan. He has issue, 2 sons:
- a) Sheikh Zayed bin Saeed
- b) Sheikh Hamdan bin Saeed

7) Sheikh Issa bin Zayed, *b.* 1966 (*s/o* Amna), *educ.* fmr Undersecretary of Abu Dhabi Public Works Department, *m.* Sheikha Mariam bint Hamdan bin Mohammed Al-Nahyan. He has issue, 5 sons and ? daughters:
- a) Sheikh Zayed bin Issa
- b) Sheikh Dhiyab bin Issa
- c) Sheikh Hamdan bin Issa
- d) Sheikh Haza'a bin Issa
- e) Sheikh Nasser bin Issa

8) Sheikh Nahyan bin Zayed, *b.* 1967 (*s/o* Aisha), *educ.* fmr Deputy Commander of the Emiri Guards, Commander of the Emiri Guards 2001, *m.*(first) Sheikha Salaama bint Mohammed bin Butti Al-Hamed, *m.* (second) Sheikha Maitha bint Mohammed bin Khaled Al-Nahyan. He has issue, 1 son and 1 daughter:
- a) Sheikh Zayed bin Nahyan
- a) Sheikha Roda bint Nahyan

9) Sheikh Saif bin Zayed, *b.* 1968 (*s/o* Moza), *educ.* UAE University (BA Political Science) Lt in Abu Dhabi Police 1990; Deputy Director of Abu Dhabi Police 1995-97; Director General 1995-1997; Undersecretary of the Ministry of Interior 1997-2004; Minister of Interior 2004-, Deputy Prime Minister, *m.* Sheikha Asma bint Awaida bin Suhail Al-Khaili. He has issue, 2 sons and 1 daughter:
- a) Sheikh Zayed bin Saif, b. 2005
- b) Sheikh Khalifa bin Saif
- a) Sheikha Moza bint Saif

10) Sheikh Nasser bin Zayed, *b.* 1968 *d.* 2008 (*s/o* Amna), *m.* ? He had issue, 1 son:
- a) Sheikh Ahmed bin Nasser

11) Sheikh Ahmed bin Zayed, *b.* 1969 *d.* 2010 (*s/o* Moza), *educ.* fmr Undersecretary of the Ministry of

Finance and Industry, fmr Chairman Abu Dhabi Investment Authority (ADIA) *m*. Sheikha Alyazia bint Hamad Al-Khaili. He had issue, 1 son:

- a) Sheikh Zayed bin Ahmed

12) Sheikh Tahnoon bin Zayed, *b*. 1969 (*s/o* Fatima), *educ*. fmr Chairman of the President's Private Department, Deputy National Security Advisor 2014, National Security Advisor 2016, *m*. 1997, Sheikha Khawla bint Ahmed Al-Suwaidi. He has issue, 1 son and 1 daughter:

- a) Sheikh Zayed bin Tahnoon
- a) Sheikha Fatima bint Tahnoon

13) Sheikh Mansour bin Zayed, *b*. 1970 (*s/o* Fatima), *educ*. UAE (BA International Affairs. 1993) Minister of Presidential Affairs 2004-, Deputy Prime Minister UAE 2009-, *m*. (first) 1994, Sheikha Alia bint Mohammed bin Butti Al-Hamed, *m*. (second) 2005, Sheikha Manal bint Mohammed bin Rashid Al-Maktoum. He has issue, 4 sons and 2 daughters:

- a) Sheikh Zayed bin Mansour (*s/o* Alia)
- b) Sheikh Mohammed bin Mansour, b. 2007 (*s/o* Manal)
- c) Sheikh Hamdan bin Mansour, b. 2011 (*s/o* Manal)
- d) Sheikh Rashid bin Mansour, b. 2017 (*s/o* Manal)
- a) Sheikha Fatima bint Mansour, b. 2006 (*d/o* Manal)
- b) Sheikha Latifa bint Mansour, b. 2014 (*d/o* Manal)

14) Sheikh Falah bin Zayed, *b*. 1970 (*s/o* Aisha), *educ. m*. (first) d. of Hamdan Boukbi Al-Mansouri (*div*), *m*. (second)? He has issue, 1 son and 2 daughters:

- a) Sheikh Sultan bin Falah, b. 2004
- a) Sheikha Layla bint Falah, b. 2004
- b) Sheikha Aisha bint Falah

15) Sheikh Hamed bin Zayed, *b*. 1971 (*s/o* Moza), *educ*. UAE University (BA Economics. 1994), University of Wales, UK (Masters Economics. 2000), Chairman of the Abu Dhabi Economic Department, Member of the Abu Dhabi Executive Council, Chief of the Abu Dhabi

Crown Prince's Court, *m.* 2002, d. of Hamad bin Suhail Al-Khaili. He has issue, 1 son and 1 daughter:
- o a) Sheikh Zayed bin Hamed
- o a) Sheikha Moza bint Hamed

16) Sheikh Dhiyab bin Zayed, *b.* 1971 (*s/o* Aisha), *educ.* UAE University (1994), fmr Director of the Presidential Court, fmr Chairman of the Abu Dhabi Water and Electricity Authority

17) Sheikh Omar bin Zayed, *b.* 1972 (*s/o* Moza), *educ.* fmr President's Aide De Camp, Deputy Chairman of the Zayed Charitable and Humanitarian Foundation, *m.* 2013 a d. of Sheikh Nahyan bin Mubarak Al-Nahyan. He has issue, 1 son:
- o a) Sheikh Zayed bin Omar, *b.* 2015

18) Sheikh Abdullah bin Zayed, *b.* 1972 (*s/o* Fatima), *educ.* UAE University (BA Political Science. 1995), Undersecretary of the UAE Ministry of Information and Culture 1995-1997, Minister of Information and Culture of the UAE March 1997-February 2006, Foreign Minister of the UAE February 2006-, *m.* 2002 Sheikha Alyazia bint Saif bin Mohammed Al-Nahyan. He has issue, 3 sons and 1 daughter:
- o a) Sheikh Mohammed bin Abdullah, *b.* 2004
- o b) Sheikh Zayed bin Abdullah
- o c) Sheikh Saif bin Abdullah
- o d) Sheikh Dhiyab bin Abdullah
- o a) Sheikha Fatima bint Abdullah

19) Sheikh Khaled bin Zayed, b. 1978 (*s/o* Moza), Chairman of the Board Zayed Higher Organization for Humanitarian Care and Special Needs

1) Sheikha Salaama bint Zayed (*d/o* the 2nd wife)
2) Sheikha Shamsa bint Zayed, *b.* 1960 (*d/o* Moza)
3) Sheikha Latifa bint Zayed, *b.* 1963 (*d/o* Aisha)
4) Sheikha Moza bint Zayed, *b.* 1964 (*d/o* Aisha)
5) Sheikha Afra bint Zayed, *b.* 1966 (*d/o* Moza)
6) Sheikha Shamma bint Zayed, *b.* 1967 (*d/o* Fatima)
7) Sheikha Alyazia bint Zayed, *b.* 1968 (*d/o* Fatima)
8) Sheikha Wadima bint Zayed, *b.* 1969 (*d/o* Aisha)
9) Sheikha Roda bint Zayed, *b.* 1970 (*d/o* Amna)
10) Sheikha Sheikha bint Zayed, *b.* 1974 (*d/o* Aisha)
11) Sheikha Maitha bint Zayed, *b.* 1976 (*d/o* Aisha)

2004 – H.H. **Sheikh Khalifa** bin Zayed Al-Nahyan, Ruler of Abu Dhabi, *b.* at Al-Ain 1948, son of H.H. Sheikh Zayed (II) bin Sultan Al-Nahyan, Ruler of Abu Dhabi by his first wife, Sheikha Hassa bint Mohammed bin Khalifa Al-Nahyan, *educ.* traditional Qur'anic education, Abu Dhabi Ruler's Representative in the Eastern Region 1966 - Appointed as Heir Apparent with the title of Crown Prince of Abu Dhabi February 1969, Head of the Department of Defense of Abu Dhabi 1969, Head of the Council of Ministers of Abu Dhabi and Minister of Defense and Finance July 1971, Deputy Prime Minister of the Federal Government December 1971, Chairman of the Abu Dhabi Executive Council 1974, Deputy Supreme Commander of the UAE Armed Forces 1976, President of the Supreme Petroleum Council, Chairman of the Board of Directors of the Abu Dhabi Investment Authority, Supreme Commander of the UAE Armed Forces November 2004-, *s.* as Ruler of Abu Dhabi on the death of his father November 2, 2004, elected President of the UAE by the Supreme Council on November 3, 2004, *m.* 1964 Sheikha Shamsa bint Suhail Al-Mazroui. He has issue, 2 sons and 6 daughters:

1) Dr. Sheikh Sultan bin Khalifa, *b.* 1965, Head of the Consultative Council for the Development of Economy and Tourism 1997, Chairman of the Court of HH The Crown Prince, *m.* (first) 1984 Sheikha Sheikha bint Saif bin Mohammed Al-Nahyan, *m.* (second) Sheikha Nayla Al-Qubaisi. He has issue, 3 sons and 6 daughters:
    - a) Sheikh Zayed bin Sultan (*s/o* Sheikha)
    - b) Sheikh Khalifa bin Sultan (*s/o* Sheikha)
    - c) Sheikh Mohammed bin Sultan (*s/o* Sheikha)
    - a) Sheikha Alyazia bint Sultan (*d/o* Sheikha)
    - b) Sheikha Hussa bint Sultan (*d/o* Sheikha)
    - c) Sheikha Shamma bint Sultan (*d/o* Sheikha)
    - d) Sheikha Roda bint Sultan (*d/o* Nayla)
    - e) Sheikha Shamsa bint Sultan (*d/o* Nayla)
    - f) Sheikha Dana bint Sultan (*d/o* Nayla)

2) Sheikh Mohammed bin Khalifa, *b.* 1972, *m.* 1999 Sheikha Alyazia bint Sultan bin Zayed Al-Nahyan. He has issue, 2 sons:
- a) Sheikh Hamdan bin Mohammed
- b) Sheikh Zayed bin Mohammed, *b.* 2004

1) Sheikha Sheikha bint Khalifa
2) Sheikha Moza bint Khalifa
3) Sheikha Aisha bint Khalifa
4) Sheikha Salaama bint Khalifa
5) Sheikha Latifa bint Khalifa
6) Sheikha Shamma bint Khalifa

Bibliographical Note

A large number of books went into the making of this one. These provided me a wealth of anecdotes and valuable material. Anyone who has read these books will see my debt to them. Chief among them, in no particular order, were the following: Malcolm C. Peck, *The United Arab Emirates: A Venture in Unity* (Boulder: Westview, 1986), Rosemarie Said Zahlan, *The Origins of the United Arab Emirates* (New York: St. Martin's Press, 1978), Frauke Heard-Bey, *From Trucial States to United Arab Emirates* (Longman, 1996), Andrea B. Rugh, *The Political Culture of Leadership in the United Arab Emirates* (New York: Palgrave MacMillan, 2007), Hendrik Van Der Meulen, "The Role of Tribal and Kinship Ties in the Politics of the United Arab Emirates" (Ph.D. thesis, Fletcher School of Law and Diplomacy, 1997).

Other works I consulted include: *J.B. Kelly, Arabia, the Gulf and the West* (New York: Basic Books, 1980), Miriam Joyce, *Ruling Shaikhs and Her Majesty's Government, 1960-1969* (London: Frank Cass, 2003), Michael Herb, *All in the Family: Absolutism, Revolution, and Democracy in the Middle Eastern Monarchies* (New York: State University of New York Press, 1999), Muhammad al-Fahim, *From Rags to Riches: A Story of Abu Dhabi* (London: Centre of Arab Studies, 1995), Donald Hawley, *The Trucial States* (London: Allen and Unwin, 1970),

Michael Cameron Dempsey, *Castles in the Sand: A City Planner in Abu Dhabi* (McFarland & Company, 2014)

Documents from the Foreign Office, held at the UK National Archives at Kew, London are conveniently assembled in the five-volume *Records of the Emirates 1961-1965* and the six-volume *Records of the Emirates 1966-1971*, both edited by Anita L.P. Burdett and published by Cambridge Archive Editions. US State Department cables from 1973-1979, reporting extensively on the UAE's first troubled decade, are available at aad.archives.gov. Many documents can also be found in the State Department's *Foreign Relations of the United States* series, available at history.state.gov. Other more recent cables, from the early 2000s, came to light during the WikiLeaks scandal. The *Middle East Eye* newspaper broke the news about Sheikh Hamdan bin Zayed's abortive coup.

Abu Dhabi was a hard nut to crack. Glossy brochures and plentiful hagiographies abound, but, as in all authoritarian societies, real information is quite another matter. I have run up a considerable debt to a handful of Emiratis who love both their country and its history, friends and strangers I have exploited ruthlessly in the search for secrets, perspective and reliable facts. All were generous with their time and knowledge, asking only that their names not be mentioned, for understandable reasons. One of them was a patient and learned guide to the genealogy of the Al-Nahyan, and without her help even the partial family tree I have included would not have been possible. Without fail, I have found Gulf women to be more broad-minded, and often more intelligent, than their men.

JCE
August 6, 2017

Rashid and Zayed:
Partners, rivals and founding fathers